LEARN F PROGRA........

WRITE CODE FROM SCRATCH IN A CLEAR & CONCISE WAY, WITH A COMPLETE BASIC COURSE. FROM BEGINNERS TO INTERMEDIATE, AN HANDS-ON PROJECT WITH EXAMPLES, TO FOLLOW STEP BY STEP

written by **WILLIAM GRAY**

Congratulation on downloading this book and thank You for doing so.

***<u>Please enjoy</u>** !*

© Copyright 2019 by **WILLIAM GRAY**
<u>*All rights reserved*</u>

No part of this publication may be reproduced, distributed, or transmitted in any form or by any means, including photocopying, recording, or other electronic or mechanical methods, or by any information storage and retrieval system without the prior written permission of the publisher, except in the case of very brief quotations embodied in critical reviews and certain other noncommercial uses permitted by copyright law.

TABLE OF CONTENTS

CHAPTER..10
   LEARN PYTHON PROGRAMMING...........10
   INTRODUCTION..................................10
   REASONS WHY THE MASSIVE POPULARITY OF PYTHON WILL REMAIN INTACT IN THE FUTURE........................14
   Supports Multiple Programming Paradigms.....14
   Doesn't Require Programmers to Write Lengthy Code...15
   Provides a Comprehensive Standard Library....16
   Effectuates Web Application Development......17
   Facilitates Development of High Quality GUI, Scientific and Numeric Applications..............18
   Simplifies Prototyping of Applications..19
   Can also be used for Mobile App Development20
   Open Source...22
CHAPTER 2..24
   HOW TO ACCEPT USER INPUTS AND DISPLAY OUTPUTS..............................24

CHAPTER 3 ... 45
HOW TO DEFINE YOUR OWN FUNCTIONS AND MODULES ... 45

CHAPTER 4 ... 58
HOW TO WRITE YOUR OWN CLASS ... 58
OBJECT ORIENTED ... 67

CHAPTER 5 ... 96
HOW TO WORK WITH EXTERNAL FILES .. 96

CHAPTER 6 ... 136
DISCOVER VARIABLES, STRINGS, INTEGERS, AND MORE TO DESIGN CONVERSATIONAL PROGRAMS ... 136

CHAPTER 7 ... 148
UNDERSTAND "GRAPHICAL USER INTERFACES" AND CREATE YOUR OWN ARCADE GAMES AND APPS ... 148

CHAPTER 8 ... 168
HOW BENEFICIAL IS DJANGO FOR THE EXISTING PYTHON DEVELOPERS ... 168
SHORTER AND CLEANER CODE ... 170
OPTIONS TO CUSTOMIZE WEB APPLICATIONS ... 171
BUILT-IN TOOLS FOR ACCOMPLISHING COMMON TASKS ... 172
A VARIETY OF PACKAGES ... 173
OBJECT-RELATIONAL MAPPER (ORM) ... 174

HUMAN READABLE URLS……………..175
DYNAMIC ADMIN INTERFACE…………..176
OPTIMIZED SECURITY……………………177
OPTION TO EXCHANGE IDEAS………….178

CHAPTER 9………………………………….180
IMPORTANT PYTHON FRAMEWORKS….180
1) Kivy……………………………………..182
2) Qt………………………………………..183
3) PyGUI…………………………………..184
4) WxPython……………………………….185
5) Django…………………………………..186
6) CherryPy……………………………….187
7) Flask……………………………………188
8) Pyramid…………………………………189
9) Web.py…………………………………190
10) TurboGears…………………………….191

CHAPTER 10…………………………………..193
ROLE OF PYTHON IN IMAGE APPLICATIONS……………………………..193

CHAPTER 11……………………………………...200
LOGISTIC REGRESSION WITH L2 REGULARIZATION IN PYTHON………….200

CHAPTER 12……………………………………..223

CAN PYTHON WEB APPLICATIONS BE TESTED USING SELENIUM?……………...223

Supports Major Operating Systems and Web Browsers…………………………………...226

Allows Users to Create Complete Test Automation Suite……………………………..227

EXECUTES TESTS FASTER………………..228

Requires Basic HTML Concepts……………..229

Helps Testers to Address Maintainability Issues……………………………………....230

Provides Selenium Python API………………231

Works with several testing frameworks…..…232

CHAPTER 13……………………………………..234

PERL AND PYTHON………………………..234

1) Design Goal………………………………236

2) Syntax Rules………………………………237

3) Family of Languages………………………238

4) Ways to Achieve Same Results……………239

5) Web Scripting Language…………………..240

6) Web Application Frameworks……………..241

7) Usage………………………………………242

8) Performance and Speed……………………243

9) Structured Data Analysis………………….244

10) JVM Interoperability……………………..245

11) Advanced Object Oriented Programming..246

12) Text Processing Capability............................247

CHAPTER 14..249

APPS BUILT WITH PYTHON..................249

Instagram..251

Pinterest..252

Disqus..253

Spotify...254

Dropbox..255

Uber...256

Reddit..257

CHAPTER 15..259

TOOLS TO RUN PYTHON ON ANDROID..259

BeeWare..261

Cha□uopy...262

Kivy...264

Pyqtdeploy..267

Qpython..269

SL4A...270

PySide...272

Termux...273

CHAPTER 16……………………………..274
PYTHON AS A MOBILE APP
DEVELOPMENT LANGUAGE…………….274

CHAPTER 17……………………………..283
PROGRAMMING LANGUAGES FOR
MOBILE APP DEVELOPMENT…………....283

BuildFire.js…………………………………...288

Python…………………………………….…..290

Java……………………………………….…..294

PHP……………………………………….…..298

Swift……………………………………….….302

C#………………………………………….….305

Objective-C……………………………….…..308

C++……………………………………….…...310

JavaScript……………………………….…….314

HTML5……………………………….……….316

Ruby……………………………….………….319

Perl………………………………….…………322

Rust………………………………….………...324

SQL……………………………….…………..327

CHAPTER 1

LEARN PYTHON PROGRAMMING

INTRODUCTION

Python is an example of a high level language. Other high level languages you might have heard of are C++,PHP,Pascal,C#,and Java. Python is an easy to learn, powerful programming language. It has efficient high-level data structures and a simple but effective approach to object-oriented programming.

Python was originally conceived by Van Rossum as a hobby language in December 1989. Also, the major and backward-incompatible version of the general-purpose programming language was released on 3rd December 2008. But Python is recently rated by a number of surveyors as the most popular coding language of 2015. The massive popularity indicates Python's effectiveness as a modern programming language. At the same time, Python 3 is currently used by developers across the worlds for creating a variety of desktop GUI, web and mobile applications.

Python is a high-level, interpreted scripting language developed in the late 1980s by Guido van Rossum at the National Research Institute for Mathematics and Computer Science in the Netherlands. The initial version was published at the alt.sources newsgroup in 1991, and version 1.0 was released in 1994.

Python 2.0 was released in 2000, and the 2.x versions were the prevalent releases until December 2008. At that time, the development team made the decision to release version 3.0, which contained a few relatively small but significant changes that were not backward compatible with the 2.x versions. Python 2 and 3 are very similar, and some features of Python 3 have been backported to Python 2. But in general, they remain not quite compatible.

Both Python 2 and 3 have continued to be maintained and developed, with periodic release updates for both. As of this writing, the most recent versions available are 2.7.15 and 3.6.5. However, an official End Of Life date of January 1, 2020 has been established for Python 2, after which time it will no longer be maintained. If you are a newcomer to Python, it is recommended that you focus on Python 3, as this tutorial will do.

Python is still maintained by a core development team at the Institute, and Guido is still in charge, having been given the title of BDFL (Benevolent Dictator For Life) by the Python community. The name Python, by the way, derives not from the snake, but from the British comedy troupe Monty Python's Flying Circus, of which Guido was, and presumably still is, a fan. It is common to find references to Monty Python sketches and movies scattered throughout the Python documentation.

There are also a number of reasons why the huge popularity and market share of Python will remain intact over a longer period of time.

REASONS WHY THE MASSIVE POPULARITY OF PYTHON WILL REMAIN INTACT IN THE FUTURE

Supports Multiple Programming Paradigms

Good developers often take advantage of different programming paradigms to reduce the amount of time and efforts required for developing large and complex applications. Like other modern programming languages, Python also supports a number of commonly used programming styles including object-oriented, functional, procedural and imperative. It further features automatic memory management, along with a dynamic type system. So programmers can use the language to effectuate development of large and complex software applications.

Doesn't Require Programmers to Write Lengthy Code

Python is designed with complete focus on code readability. So the programmers can create readable code base that can be used by members of distributed teams. At the same time, the simple syntax of the programming language enables them to express concepts without writing longer lines of code. The feature makes it easier for developers to large and complex applications within a stipulated amount of time. As they can easily skip certain tasks required by other programming languages, it becomes easier for developers to maintain and update their applications.

Provides a Comprehensive Standard Library

Python further scores over other programming languages due to its extensive standard library. The programmers can use these libraries to accomplish a variety of tasks without writing longer lines of code. Also, the standard library of Python is designed with a large number of high use programming tasks scripted into it. Thus, it helps programmers to accomplish tasks like string operations, development and implementation of web services, working with internet protocols, and handling operating system interface.

Effectuates Web Application Development

Python is designed as a general-purpose programming language, and lacks built-in web development features. But the web developers use a variety of add-on modules to write modern web applications in Python. While writing web applications in Python, programmers have option to use several high-level web frameworks including Django, web2py, TurboGears, CubicWeb, and Reahl. These web frameworks help programmers to perform a number of operations, without writing additional code, like database manipulation, URL routing, session storage and retrieval, and output template formatting. They can further use the web frameworks to protect the web application from cross-site scripting attacks, SQL injection, and cross-site request forgery.

Facilitates Development of High Quality GUI, Scientific and Numeric Applications

Python is currently available on major operating systems like Windows, Mac OS X, Linux and UNIX. So the desktop GUI applications written in the programming language can be deployed on multiple platforms. The programmers can further speedup cross-platform desktop GUI application development using frameworks like Kivy, wxPython and PyGtk. A number of reports have highlighted that Python is used widely for development of numeric and scientific applications. While writing scientific and numeric applications in Python, the developers can take advantage of tools like Scipy, Pandas, IPython, along with the Python Imaging Library.

Simplifies Prototyping of Applications

Nowadays, each organization wants to beat competition by developing software with distinct and innovative features. That is why; prototyping has become an integral part of modern software development lifecycle. Before writing the code, developers have to create prototype of the application to display its features and functionality to various stakeholders. As a simple and fast programming language, Python enables programmers to develop the final system without putting any extra time and effort. At the same time, the developers also have option to start developing the system directly from the prototype simply by refactoring the code.

Can also be used for Mobile App Development

Frameworks like Kivy also make Python usable for developing mobile apps. As a library, Kivy can be used for creating both desktop applications and mobile apps. But it allows developers to write the code once, and deploy the same code on multiple platforms. Along with interfacing with the hardware of the mobile device, Kivy also comes with built-in camera adapters, modules to render and play videos, and modules to accept user input through multi-touch and gestures. Thus, programmers can use Kivy to create different versions of the same applications for iOS, Android and Windows Phone. Also, the framework does not require developers to write longer lines of code while creating Kivy programs. After creating different versions of the mobile app, they can package the app separately for individual app store. The option makes it easier for developers to create different versions of the mobile app without deploying separate developers.

Open Source

Despite being rated as the most popular coding language of 2015, Python is still available as open source and free software. Along with large IT companies, the startups and freelance software developers can also use the programming language without paying any fees or royalty. Thus, Python makes it easier for businesses to reduce development cost significantly. At the same time, the programmers can also avail the assistance of large and active community to add out-of-box features to the software application.

The last major release of Python took place in December 2008. Python 3 was released as a backward-incompatible version with most of the major features back ported to Python 2.6 and 2.7. However, the programming language is being updated by the community at regular intervals. The community released Python 3.4.3 on 23rd

February with several features and patches. So the developer can always use the most recent version of the Python programming language to effectuate development of various software applications.

CHAPTER 2

HOW TO ACCEPT USER INPUTS AND DISPLAY OUTPUTS

The Input Function

The hello program of The Classic First Program always does the same thing. This is not very interesting. Programs are only going to be reused if they can act on a variety of data. One way to get data is directly from the user. Modify the hello.py program as follows in the editor, and save it with File ▸ Save As....`, using the name hello_you.py.

person = input('Enter your name: ')
print('Hello', person)
Run the program. In the Shell you should see

Enter your name:

Follow the instruction (and press Enter). Make sure the typing cursor is in the Shell window, at the end of this line. After you type your response, you can see that the program has taken in the line you typed. That is what the built-in function input does: First it prints the string you give as a parameter (in this case 'Enter your name: '), and then it waits for a line to be typed in, and returns the string of characters you typed. In the hello_you.py program this value is assigned to the variable person, for use later.

The parameter inside the parentheses after input is important. It is a prompt, prompting you that keyboard input is expected at that point, and hopefully indicating what is being requested. Without the prompt, the user would not know what was happening, and the computer would just sit there waiting!

Open the example program, interview.py. Before running it (with any made-up data), see if you can figure out what it will do:

"'Illustrate input and print.'"

applicant = input("Enter the applicant's name: ")
interviewer = input("Enter the interviewer's name: ")
time = input("Enter the appointment time: ")
print(interviewer, "will interview", applicant, "at", time)

The statements are executed in the order they appear in the text of the program: sequentially. This is the simplest way for the execution of the program to flow. You will see instructions later that alter that natural flow.

If we want to reload and modify the hello_you.py program to put an exclamation point at the end, you could try:

```
person = input('Enter your name: ')
print('Hello', person, '!')
```

Run it and you see that it is not spaced right. There should be no space after the person's name, but the default behavior of the print function is to have each field printed separated by a space. There are several ways to fix this. You should know one. Think about it before going on to the next section. Hint: [1]

[1] The + operation on strings adds no extra space.

1.10.2. Print with Keyword Parameter sep

One way to put punctuation but no space after the person in hello_you.py is to use the plus operator, +. Another approach is to change the default separator between fields in the print function. This will introduce a new syntax feature, keyword parameters. The print function has a keyword parameter named sep. If you leave it out of a call to print, as we have so far, it is set equal to a space by default. If you add a final field, sep='', in the print function in hello_you.py, you get the following example file, hello_you2.py:

```
'''Hello to you!  Illustrates sep with empty string in print.
'''

person = input('Enter your name: ')
print('Hello ', person, '!', sep='')
```

Try the program.

Keyword paramaters must be listed at the end of the parameter list.

1.10.3. Numbers and Strings of Digits

Consider the following problem: Prompt the user for two numbers, and then print out a sentence stating the sum. For instance if the user entered 2 and 3, you would print 'The sum of 2 and 3 is 5.'

You might imagine a solution like the example file addition1.py, shown below. There is a problem. Can you figure it out before you try it? Hint: [2]

'"Error in addition from input."'

```
x = input("Enter a number: ")
y = input("Enter a second number: ")
print('The sum of ', x, ' and ', y, ' is ', x+y, '.',
sep='') #error
```

End up running it in any case.

We do not want string concatenation, but integer addition. We need integer operands. Briefly mentioned in Whirlwind Introduction To Types and Functions was the fact that we can use type names as functions to convert types. One approach would be to do that. Further variable names are also introduced in the example addition2.py file below to emphasize the distinctions in types. Read and run:

```
'''Conversion of strings to int before addition'''

xString = input("Enter a number: ")
x = int(xString)
yString = input("Enter a second number: ")
y = int(yString)
print('The sum of ', x, ' and ', y, ' is ', x+y, '.',
sep='')
```

Needing to convert string input to numbers is a common situation, both with keyboard input and later in web pages. While the extra variables above emphasized the steps, it is more concise to write as in the variation in example file, addition3.py, doing the conversions to type int immediately:

'''Two numeric inputs, with immediate conversion'''

```
x = int(input("Enter a number: "))
y = int(input("Enter a second number: "))
print('The sum of ', x, ' and ', y, ' is ', x+y, '.',
sep='')
```

The simple programs so far have followed a basic programming pattern: input-calculate-output. Get all the data first, calculate with it second, and output the results last. The pattern sequence would be even clearer if we explicitly create a named result variable in the middle, as in addition4.py

```
'''Two numeric inputs, explicit sum'''

x = int(input("Enter an integer: "))
y = int(input("Enter another integer: "))
sum = x+y

print('The sum of ', x, ' and ', y, ' is ', sum, '.', sep='')
```

We will see more complicated patterns, which involve repetition, in the future.

[2] The input function produces values of string type.

1.10.3.1. Exercise for Addition

Write a version, add3.py, that asks for three numbers, and lists all three, and their sum, in similar format to addition4.py displayed above.

1.10.3.2. Exercise for Quotients

Write a program, quotient.py, that prompts the user for two integers, and then prints them out in a sentence with an integer division problem like

The quotient of 14 and 3 is 4 with a remainder of 2

Review Division and Remainders if you forget the integer division or remainder operator.

1.10.4. String Format Operation

In grade school quizzes a common convention is to use fill-in-the blanks. For instance,

Hello _____!

and you can fill in the name of the person greeted, and combine given text with a chosen insertion. We use this as an analogy: Python has a similar construction, better called fill-in-the-braces. There is a particular operation on strings called format, that makes substitutions into places enclosed in braces. For instance the example file, hello_you3.py, creates and prints the same string as in hello_you2.py from the previous section:

'''Hello to you! Illustrates format with {} in print.
'''

person = input('Enter your name: ')
greeting = 'Hello, {}!'.format(person)
print(greeting)

There are several new ideas here!

First method calling syntax for objects is used. You will see this very important modern syntax in more detail at the beginning of the next chapter in

Object Orientation. All data in Python are objects, including strings. Objects have a special syntax for functions, called methods, associated with the particular type of object. In particular str objects have a method called format. The syntax for methods has the object followed by a period followed by the method name, and further parameters in parentheses.

object.methodname(parameters)

In the example above, the object is the string 'Hello {}!'. The method is named format. There is one further parameter, person.

The string for the format method has a special form, with braces embedded. Places where braces are embedded are replaced by the value of an expression taken from the parameter list for the format method. There are many variations on the syntax between the braces. In this case we use the syntax where the first (and only) location in the string with braces has a substitution made from the first (and only) parameter.

In the code above, this new string is assigned to the identifier greeting, and then the string is printed.

The identifier greeting was introduced to break the operations into a clearer sequence of steps. However, since the value of greeting is only referenced once, it can be eliminated with the more concise version:

person = input('Enter your name: ')
print('Hello {}!'.format(person))

Consider the interview program. Suppose we want to add a period at the end of the sentence (with no space before it). One approach would be to combine everything with plus signs. Another way is printing with keyword sep=''. Another approach is with string formatting. Using our grade school analogy, the idea is to fill in the blanks in

_____ will interview _____ at _____.

There are multiple places to substitute, and the format approach can be extended to multiple substitutions: Each place in the format string where there is '{}', the format operation will substitute the value of the next parameter in the format parameter list.

Run the example file interview2.py, and check that the results from all three methods match.

'''Compare print with concatenation and with format string.'''

applicant = input("Enter the applicant's name: ")

```
interviewer = input("Enter the interviewer's name: ")
time = input("Enter the appointment time: ")
print(interviewer + ' will interview ' + applicant +
' at ' + time +'.')
print(interviewer, ' will interview ', applicant, ' at ',
time, '.', sep='')
print('{} will interview {} at {}.'.format(interviewer, applicant, time))
```

Sometimes you want a single string, but not just for printing. You can combine pieces with the + operator, but then all pieces must be strings or explicitly converted to strings. An advantage of the format method is that it will convert types to string automatically, like the print function. Here is another variant of our addition sentence example, addition4a.py, using the format method.

'''Two numeric inputs, explicit sum'''

```
x = int(input("Enter an integer: "))
y = int(input("Enter another integer: "))
sum = x+y
sentence = 'The sum of {} and {} is {}.'.format(x, y, sum)
print(sentence)
```

Conversion to strings was not needed in interview2.py. (Everything started out as a string.) In addition4a.py, however, the automatic conversion of the integers to strings is useful.

So far there is no situation that requires a format string instead of using other approaches. Sometimes a format string provides a shorter and simpler expression. Except where specifically instructed in an exercise for practice, use whatever approach to combining strings and data that you like. There are many elaborations to the fields in braces to control formatting. We will look at one later, String Formats for Float Precision, where format strings are particularly useful.

A technical point: Since braces have special meaning in a format string, there must be a special rule if you want braces to actually be included in the final formatted string. The rule is to double the braces: '{{' and '}}'. The example code formatBraces.py, shown below, makes setStr refer to the string 'The set is {5,9}.'. The initial and final doubled braces in the format string generate literal braces in the formatted string:

'''Illustrate braces in a formatted string.'''

a = 5
b = 9
setStr = 'The set is {{{}, {}}}.'.format(a, b)
print(setStr)

This kind of format string depends directly on the order of the parameters to the format method. There is another approach with a dictionary, that was used in the first sample program, madlib.py, and will be discussed more in Dictionaries and String Formatting. The dictionary approach is probably the best in many cases, but the count-based approach is an easier start, particularly if the parameters are just used once, in order.

Optional elaboration with explicitly numbered entries

Imagine the format parameters numbered in order, starting from 0. In this case 0, 1, and 2. The number of the parameter position may be included inside the braces, so an alternative to the last line of interview2.py is (added in example file interview3.py):

```python
print('{0} will interview {1} at {2}.'.format(interviewer, applicant, time))
```

This is more verbose than the previous version, with no obvious advantage. However, if you desire to use some of the parameters more than once, then the approach with the numerical identification with the parameters is useful. Every place the string includes '{0}', the format operation will substitute the value of the initial parameter in the list. Wherever '{1}' appears, the next format parameter will be substituted....

Predict the results of the example file arith.py shown below, if you enter 5 and 6. Then check yourself by running it. In this case the numbers referring to the parameter positions are necessary. They are both repeated and used out of order:

```
'''Fancier format string example with
parameter identification numbers
-- useful when some parameters are used several times.'''

x = int(input('Enter an integer: '))
y = int(input('Enter another integer: '))
formatStr = '{0} + {1} = {2}; {0} * {1} = {3}.'
equations = formatStr.format(x, y, x+y, x*y)
print(equations)
```

Try the program with other data.

Now that you have a few building blocks, you will see more exercises where you need to start to do creative things. You are encouraged to go back and reread Learning to Problem-Solve.

1.10.4.1. Addition Format Exercise

Write a version of Exercise for Addition, add3f.py, that uses the string format method to construct the same final string as before.

1.10.4.2. Quotient Format Exercise

Write a version of the quotient problem in Exercise for Quotients, quotientformat.py, that uses the string format method to construct the same final string as before. Again be sure to give a full sentence stating both the integer quotient and the remainder.

CHAPTER 3

HOW TO DEFINE YOUR OWN FUNCTIONS AND MODULES

Modules refer to a file containing Python statements and definitions.

A file containing Python code, for e.g.: example.py, is called a module and its module name would be example.

We use modules to break down large programs into small manageable and organized files. Furthermore, modules provide reusability of code.

We can define our most used functions in a module and import it, instead of copying their definitions into different programs.

Let us create a module. Type the following and save it as example.py.

\# Python Module example

```
def add(a, b):
   """This program adds two
   numbers and return the result"""

   result = a + b
   return result
```

Here, we have defined a function add() inside a module named example. The function takes in two numbers and returns their sum.

How to import modules in Python?

We can import the definitions inside a module to another module or the interactive interpreter in Python.

We use the import keyword to do this. To import our previously defined module example we type the following in the Python prompt.

>>> import example

This does not enter the names of the functions defined in example directly in the current symbol table. It only enters the module name example there.

Using the module name we can access the function using the dot . operator. For example:

>>> example.add(4,5.5)

9.5

Python has a ton of standard modules available.

You can check out the full list of Python standard modules and what they are for. These files are in the Lib directory inside the location where you installed Python.

Standard modules can be imported the same way as we import our user-defined modules.

There are various ways to import modules. They are listed as follows.

Python import statement

We can import a module using import statement and access the definitions inside it using the dot operator as described above. Here is an example.

\# import statement example
\# to import standard module math

import math)
print("The value of pi is", math.pi

When you run the program, the output will be:

The value of pi is 3.141592653589793

Import with renaming

We can import a module by renaming it as follows.

\# import module by renaming it

import math as m
print("The value of pi is", m.pi)

We have renamed the math module as m. This can save us typing time in some cases.

Note that the name math is not recognized in our scope. Hence, math.pi is invalid, m.pi is the correct implementation.

Python from...import statement

We can import specific names from a module without importing the module as a whole. Here is an example.

```
# import only pi from math module
```

```
from math import pi
print("The value of pi is", pi)
```

We imported only the attribute pi from the module.

In such case we don't use the dot operator. We could have imported multiple attributes as

```
>>> from math import pi, e
>>> pi
3.141592653589793
>>> e
2.718281828459045
```

Import all names
We can import all names(definitions) from a module using the following construct.

```python
# import all names from the standard module math

from math import *
print("The value of pi is", pi)
```

We imported all the definitions from the math module. This makes all names except those beginnig with an underscore, visible in our scope.

Importing everything with the asterisk (*) symbol is not a good programming practice. This can lead to duplicate definitions for an identifier. It also hampers the readability of our code.

Python Module Search Path
While importing a module, Python looks at several places. Interpreter first looks for a built-in module then (if not found) into a list of directories defined in sys.path. The search is in this order.

The current directory.

PYTHONPATH (an environment variable with a list of directory).

The installation-dependent default directory.

```
>>> import sys
>>> sys.path
['',
'C:\\Python33\\Lib\\idlelib',
'C:\\Windows\\system32\\python33.zip',
'C:\\Python33\\DLLs',
'C:\\Python33\\lib',
'C:\\Python33',
'C:\\Python33\\lib\\site-packages']
```

We can add modify this list to add our own path.

Reloading a module

The Python interpreter imports a module only once during a session. This makes things more efficient. Here is an example to show how this works.

Suppose we have the following code in a module named my_module.

```
# This module shows the effect of
#  multiple imports and reload

print("This code got executed")
```

Now we see the effect of multiple imports.

```
>>> import my_module
This code got executed
>>> import my_module
>>> import my_module
```

We can see that our code got executed only once. This goes to say that our module was imported only once.

Now if our module changed during the course of the program, we would have to reload it. One way to do this is to restart the interpreter. But this does not help much.

Python provides a neat way of doing this. We can use the reload() function inside the imp module to reload a module. This is how its done.

>>> import imp
>>> import my_module
This code got executed
>>> import my_module
>>> imp.reload(my_module)
This code got executed
<module 'my_module' from '.\\my_module.py'>
The dir() built-in function
We can use the dir() function to find out names that are defined inside a module.

For example, we have defined a function add() in the module example that we had in the beginning.

```
>>> dir(example)
['__builtins__',
'__cached__',
'__doc__',
'__file__',
'__initializing__',
'__loader__',
'__name__',
'__package__',
'add']
```

Here, we can see a sorted list of names (along with add). All other names that begin with an underscore are default Python attributes associated with the module (we did not define them ourself).

For example, the __name__ attribute contains the name of the module.

```
>>> import example
>>> example.__name__
'example'
```

All the names defined in our current namespace can be found out using the dir() function without any arguments.

```
>>> a = 1
>>> b = "hello"
>>> import math
>>> dir()
['__builtins__', '__doc__', '__name__', 'a', 'b', 'math', 'pyscripter']
```

Check out these examples to learn more:

Python Program to Shuffle Deck of Cards
Python Program to Display Calendar.

CHAPTER 4

HOW TO WRITE YOUR OWN CLASS

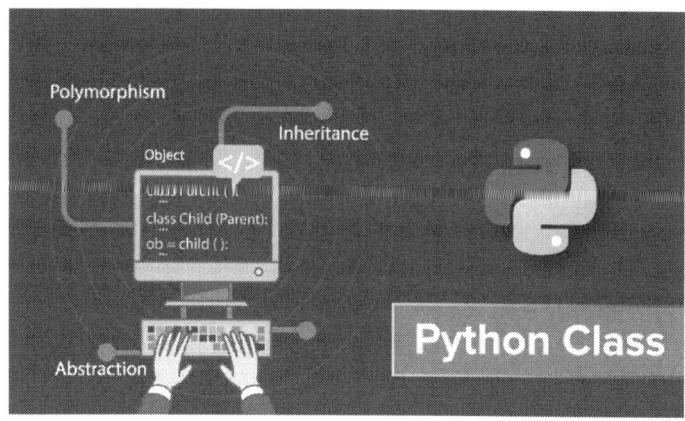

In object-oriented computer languages such as Python, classes are basically a template to create your own objects. Objects are an encapsulation of variables and functions into a single entity. Objects get their variables and functions from classes.

Here are some examples that will help you understand—read on. There is also an interactive code shell, simply press the "Run" button at the top of the specific window.

The simplest way to describe classes and how to use them is this:

Imagine you have great powers. You create a species ("class").

Then you create attributes for that species ("properties")—height, weight, limbs, color, powers, and so on.

Then you create an instance of that species—Fido the dog, Drogon from Game of Thrones, and so on. Then you work with these instances:

In a game, for instance, they would engage in action, interact, using their attributes.
In a banking app, they would be the different transactions.
In a vehicle buy/sell/trade/lease app, the vehicle class could then spawn sub-classes such as cars.

Each would have attributes such as mileage, options, features, color, and trim.

You can already see why this is useful. You are creating, re-using, adapting, and enhancing items in a very efficient, logical, and useful way.

By now, you have probably realized that this is a way to classify and group, one that that is similar to how humans learn:

Animals are living things that are not human or trees, in a basic sense

then you move on to different types of animals— dogs, cats are probably the first animals most of us learnt about

then you move to different attributes of animals— shapes, sizes, sounds, appendages and so on.

For instance, when you were a child, your first understanding of a dog was probably something with four legs that barked. Then you learnt to distinguish that some were real dogs, others were toys. That this "dog" concept contained many types.

Creating and using classes is basically:

building a template to put "things" in—a classification
which can then be operated on. For example, pulling up all the people with dogs that you could request to link to a blog on pets, or all bank clients who might be good prospects for a new credit card.

The main point here is classes are objects that can produce instances of those templates, on which operations and methods can be applied. It is an excellent way to conceptualize, organize, and build a hierarchy for any organization or process.

As our world gets more complex, this is a way to mimic that complexity from a hierarchical perspective. It also builds a deeper understanding of the processes and interactions for business, technical, and social settings from a virtual information technology point.

An example might be a video game you create. Each character could be a "class", with its own attributes, that interacts with instances of other classes. King George of the "King" class might interact with Court Jester Funnyman of the "Clown" class, and so on. A King might have a royal "servant" class, and a "servant" class would always have a "King" class, for example.

This is what we will do:

create a class and use it

create a module and move the class creation and initiation to the module

call the module in a new program to use the class.

```
#TSB - Create Class in Python - rocket positions (x,y) and graph
#some items and comments bolded to call attention to process
import matplotlib.pyplot as plt
class Rocket():
  def __init__(self, x=0, y=0):
    #each rocket has (x,y) position; user or calling function has choice
    #of passing in x and y values, or by default they are set at 0
    self.x = x
    self.y = y
```

```python
def move_up(self):
    self.y += 1

def move_down(self):
    self.y -= 1

def move_right(self):
    self.x += 1

def move_left(self):
    self.x -= 1
#Make a series of rockets - x,y positions, I am calling it rocket
rockets=[]
rockets.append(Rocket())
rockets.append(Rocket(0,2))
rockets.append(Rocket(1,4))
rockets.append(Rocket(2,6))
rockets.append(Rocket(3,7))
rockets.append(Rocket(5,9))
rockets.append(Rocket(8, 15))
```

```python
#Show on a graph where each rocket is
for index, rocket in enumerate(rockets):
    #original position of rockets
    print("Rocket %d is at (%d, %d)." % (index, rocket.x, rocket.y))
    plt.plot(rocket.x, rocket.y, 'ro', linewidth=2, linestyle='dashed', markersize=12)
    #move the 'rocket' one up
    rocket.move_up()
    print("New Rocket position %d is at (%d, %d)." % (index, rocket.x, rocket.y))
    #plot the new position
    plt.plot(rocket.x, rocket.y, 'bo', linewidth=2, linestyle='dashed', markersize=12)
    #move the rocket left, then plot the new position
    rocket.move_left()
    plt.plot(rocket.x, rocket.y, 'yo', linewidth=2, linestyle='dashed', markersize=12)
#show graph legend to match colors with position
```

```
plt.gca().legend(('original position','^ - Moved up',
'< - Moved left'))
plt.show()
#plt.legend(loc='upper left')
```

So there you have it. You can create many different classes, with parent classes, sub-classes and so on.

OBJECT ORIENTED

Python has been an object-oriented language since it existed. Because of this, creating and using classes and objects are downright easy. This chapter helps you become an expert in using Python's object-oriented programming support.

If you do not have any previous experience with object-oriented (OO) programming, you may want to consult an introductory course on it or at least a tutorial of some sort so that you have a grasp of the basic concepts.

However, here is small introduction of Object-Oriented Programming (OOP) to bring you at speed −

Overview of OOP Terminology
Class − A user-defined prototype for an object that defines a set of attributes that characterize

any object of the class. The attributes are data members (class variables and instance variables) and methods, accessed via dot notation.

Class variable – A variable that is shared by all instances of a class. Class variables are defined within a class but outside any of the class's methods. Class variables are not used as frequently as instance variables are.

Data member – A class variable or instance variable that holds data associated with a class and its objects.

Function overloading – The assignment of more than one behavior to a particular function. The operation performed varies by the types of objects or arguments involved.

Instance variable – A variable that is defined inside a method and belongs only to the current instance of a class.

Inheritance – The transfer of the characteristics of a class to other classes that are derived from it.

Instance – An individual object of a certain class. An object obj that belongs to a class Circle, for example, is an instance of the class Circle.

Instantiation – The creation of an instance of a class.

Method – A special kind of function that is defined in a class definition.

Object – A unique instance of a data structure that's defined by its class. An object comprises both data members (class variables and instance variables) and methods.

Operator overloading − The assignment of more than one function to a particular operator.

Creating Classes

The class statement creates a new class definition. The name of the class immediately follows the keyword class followed by a colon as follows −

class ClassName:
   'Optional class documentation string'
   class_suite

The class has a documentation string, which can be accessed via ClassName.__doc__.

The class_suite consists of all the component statements defining class members, data attributes and functions.

Example

Following is the example of a simple Python class −

```
class Employee:
   'Common base class for all employees'
   empCount = 0

   def __init__(self, name, salary):
      self.name = name
      self.salary = salary
      Employee.empCount += 1

   def displayCount(self):
     print "Total Employee %d" % Employee.empCount

   def displayEmployee(self):
      print "Name : ", self.name,  ", Salary: ", self.salary
```

The variable empCount is a class variable whose value is shared among all instances of a this class. This can be accessed as Employee.empCount from inside the class or outside the class.

The first method __init__() is a special method, which is called class constructor or initialization method that Python calls when you create a new instance of this class.

You declare other class methods like normal functions with the exception that the first argument to each method is self. Python adds the self argument to the list for you; you do not need to include it when you call the methods.

Creating Instance Objects
To create instances of a class, you call the class using class name and pass in whatever arguments its __init__ method accepts.

"This would create first object of Employee class"

emp1 = Employee("Zara", 2000)

"This would create second object of Employee class"

emp2 = Employee("Manni", 5000)

Accessing Attributes

You access the object's attributes using the dot operator with object. Class variable would be accessed using class name as follows −

emp1.displayEmployee()

emp2.displayEmployee()

print "Total Employee %d" % Employee.empCount

Now, putting all the concepts together:

#!/usr/bin/python

class Employee:
    'Common base class for all employees'

```python
    empCount = 0

    def __init__(self, name, salary):
        self.name = name
        self.salary = salary
        Employee.empCount += 1

    def displayCount(self):
        print "Total Employee %d" % Employee.empCount

    def displayEmployee(self):
        print "Name : ", self.name,  ", Salary: ", self.salary

"This would create first object of Employee class"
emp1 = Employee("Zara", 2000)
"This would create second object of Employee class"
emp2 = Employee("Manni", 5000)
emp1.displayEmployee()
```

emp2.displayEmployee()

print "Total Employee %d" %
Employee.empCount

When the above code is executed, it produces the following result −

Name : Zara ,Salary: 2000

Name : Manni ,Salary: 5000

Total Employee 2

You can add, remove, or modify attributes of classes and objects at any time −

emp1.age = 7 # Add an 'age' attribute.

emp1.age = 8 # Modify 'age' attribute.

del emp1.age # Delete 'age' attribute.

Instead of using the normal statements to access attributes, you can use the following functions −

The getattr(obj, name[, default]) − to access the attribute of object.

The hasattr(obj,name) − to check if an attribute exists or not.

The setattr(obj,name,value) − to set an attribute. If attribute does not exist, then it would be created.

The delattr(obj, name) − to delete an attribute.

hasattr(emp1, 'age')   # Returns true if 'age' attribute exists
getattr(emp1, 'age')   # Returns value of 'age' attribute
setattr(emp1, 'age', 8) # Set attribute 'age' at 8
delattr(empl, 'age')   # Delete attribute 'age'

Built-In Class Attributes

Every Python class keeps following built-in attributes and they can be accessed using dot operator like any other attribute −

__dict__ − Dictionary containing the class's namespace.

__doc__ − Class documentation string or none, if undefined.

__name__ − Class name.

__module__ − Module name in which the class is defined. This attribute is "__main__" in interactive mode.

__bases__ − A possibly empty tuple containing the base classes, in the order of their occurrence in the base class list.

For the above class let us try to access all these attributes:

#!/usr/bin/python

class Employee:
   'Common base class for all employees'

```python
   empCount = 0

   def __init__(self, name, salary):
      self.name = name
      self.salary = salary
      Employee.empCount += 1

   def displayCount(self):
     print "Total Employee %d" % Employee.empCount

   def displayEmployee(self):
      print "Name : ", self.name,  ", Salary: ", self.salary

print "Employee.__doc__:", Employee.__doc__
print "Employee.__name__:", Employee.__name__
print "Employee.__module__:", Employee.__module__
```

print "Employee.__bases__:",
Employee.__bases__
print "Employee.__dict__:", Employee.__dict__

When the above code is executed, it produces the following result −

Employee.__doc__ : Common base class for all employees
Employee.__name__ : Employee
Employee.__module__ : __main__
Employee.__bases__ : ()
Employee.__dict__ : {'__module__': '__main__', 'displayCount':
<function displayCount at 0xb7c84994>,
'empCount': 2,
'displayEmployee': <function displayEmployee at 0xb7c8441c>,
'__doc__': 'Common base class for all employees',
'__init__': <function __init__ at 0xb7c846bc>}

Destroying Objects (Garbage Collection)

Python deletes unneeded objects (built-in types or class instances) automatically to free the memory space. The process by which Python periodically reclaims blocks of memory that no longer are in use is termed Garbage Collection.

Python's garbage collector runs during program execution and is triggered when an object's reference count reaches zero. An object's reference count changes as the number of aliases that point to it changes.

An object's reference count increases when it is assigned a new name or placed in a container (list, tuple, or dictionary). The object's reference count decreases when it's deleted with del, its reference is reassigned, or its reference goes out of scope. When an object's reference count reaches zero, Python collects it automatically.

```
a = 40     # Create object <40>
b = a      # Increase ref. count  of <40>
c = [b]    # Increase ref. count  of <40>


del a      # Decrease ref. count  of <40>
b = 100    # Decrease ref. count  of <40>
c[0] = -1  # Decrease ref. count  of <40>
```

You normally will not notice when the garbage collector destroys an orphaned instance and reclaims its space. But a class can implement the special method __del__(), called a destructor, that is invoked when the instance is about to be destroyed. This method might be used to clean up any non memory resources used by an instance.

Example

This __del__() destructor prints the class name of an instance that is about to be destroyed −

```
#!/usr/bin/python

class Point:
   def __init__( self, x=0, y=0):
      self.x = x
      self.y = y
   def __del__(self):
      class_name = self.__class__.__name__
      print class_name, "destroyed"

pt1 = Point()
pt2 = pt1
pt3 = pt1
print id(pt1), id(pt2), id(pt3) # prints the ids of the obejcts
del pt1
del pt2
```

del pt3

When the above code is executed, it produces following result −

3083401324 3083401324 3083401324

Point destroyed

Note − Ideally, you should define your classes in separate file, then you should import them in your main program file using import statement.

Class Inheritance

Instead of starting from scratch, you can create a class by deriving it from a preexisting class by listing the parent class in parentheses after the new class name.

The child class inherits the attributes of its parent class, and you can use those attributes as if they were defined in the child class. A child class can also override data members and methods from the parent.

Syntax

Derived classes are declared much like their parent class; however, a list of base classes to inherit from is given after the class name −

```
class SubClassName (ParentClass1[, ParentClass2, ...]):
   'Optional class documentation string'
   class_suite
```

```
#!/usr/bin/python

class Parent:        # define parent class
   parentAttr = 100
   def __init__(self):
      print "Calling parent constructor"

   def parentMethod(self):
      print 'Calling parent method'

   def setAttr(self, attr):
```

```
      Parent.parentAttr = attr

   def getAttr(self):
      print "Parent attribute :", Parent.parentAttr

class Child(Parent): # define child class
   def __init__(self):
      print "Calling child constructor"

   def childMethod(self):
      print 'Calling child method'

c = Child()          # instance of child
c.childMethod()      # child calls its method
c.parentMethod()     # calls parent's method
c.setAttr(200)       # again call parent's method
c.getAttr()          # again call parent's method
```

When the above code is executed, it produces the following result −

Calling child constructor

Calling child method

Calling parent method

Parent attribute : 200

Similar way, you can drive a class from multiple parent classes as follows −

class A: # define your class A
.....

class B: # define your class B
.....

class C(A, B):   # subclass of A and B
.....

You can use issubclass() or isinstance() functions to check a relationships of two classes and instances.

The issubclass(sub, sup) boolean function returns true if the given subclass sub is indeed a subclass of the superclass sup.

The isinstance(obj, Class) boolean function returns true if obj is an instance of class Class or is an instance of a subclass of Class

Overriding Methods

You can always override your parent class methods. One reason for overriding parent's methods is because you may want special or different functionality in your subclass.

Example

```
#!/usr/bin/python

class Parent:      # define parent class
   def myMethod(self):
      print 'Calling parent method'

class Child(Parent): # define child class
   def myMethod(self):
      print 'Calling child method'

c = Child()        # instance of child
c.myMethod()       # child calls overridden method
```

When the above code is executed, it produces the following result −

Calling child method

Base Overloading Methods

Following table lists some generic functionality that you can override in your own classes −

Sr.No. Method, Description & Sample Call

1

__init__ (self [,args...])

Constructor (with any optional arguments)

Sample Call : obj = className(args)

2

__del__(self)

Destructor, deletes an object

Sample Call : del obj

3

__repr__(self)

Evaluable string representation

Sample Call : repr(obj)

4
__str__(self)

Printable string representation

Sample Call : str(obj)

5
__cmp__ (self, x)

Object comparison

Sample Call : cmp(obj, x)

Overloading Operators

Suppose you have created a Vector class to represent two-dimensional vectors, what happens when you use the plus operator to add them? Most likely Python will yell at you.

You could, however, define the __add__ method in your class to perform vector addition and then the plus operator would behave as per expectation –

Example

```
#!/usr/bin/python

class Vector:
   def __init__(self, a, b):
      self.a = a
      self.b = b

   def __str__(self):
      return 'Vector (%d, %d)' % (self.a, self.b)

   def __add__(self,other):
      return Vector(self.a + other.a, self.b + other.b)

v1 = Vector(2,10)
v2 = Vector(5,-2)
print v1 + v2
```

When the above code is executed, it produces the following result −

Vector(7,8)

Data Hiding

An object's attributes may or may not be visible outside the class definition. You need to name attributes with a double underscore prefix, and those attributes then are not be directly visible to outsiders.

Example

```
#!/usr/bin/python

class JustCounter:
   __secretCount = 0

   def count(self):
      self.__secretCount += 1
      print self.__secretCount

counter = JustCounter()
counter.count()
counter.count()
print counter.__secretCount
```

When the above code is executed, it produces the following result −

1
2
Traceback (most recent call last):

    File "test.py", line 12, in <module>
        print counter.__secretCount
AttributeError: JustCounter instance has no attribute '__secretCount'

Python protects those members by internally changing the name to include the class name. You can access such attributes as object._className__attrName. If you would replace your last line as following, then it works for you −

....
print counter._JustCounter__secretCount.

CHAPTER 5

HOW TO WORK WITH EXTERNAL FILES

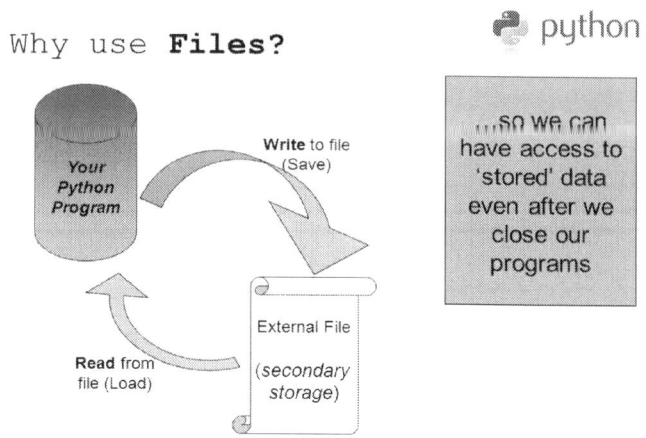

All programs must deal with external data. They will either accept data from sources outside the text of the program, or they will produce some kind of output, or they will do both. Think about it: if the program produces no output, how do you know it did anything?

By external data, we mean data outside of volatile, high-speed, primary memory; we mean data on peripheral devices. This may be persistent data on a disk, or transient data on a network interface. For now, it may mean transient data displayed on our terminal.

Most operating systems provide simple, uniform access to external data via the abstraction called a file. We'll look at the operating system implementation, as well as the Python class that gives us access to the operating system file in our programs.

In File Objects – Our Connection To The File System, we provide definitions of how Python works with files. We cover the built-in functions for working with files in The File and Open Functions. In Methods We Use on File Objects, we describe some method functions of file objects. We'll look at file-processing statements in File Statements: Reading and Writing (but no Arithmetic).

File Objects – Our Connection To The File System

Abstractions Built on Top of Abstractions. Files do a huge number of things for us. To support this broad spectrum of capabilities, there are two layers of abstraction involved: the OS and Python. Unfortunately, both layers use the same words, so we have to be careful about casually misusing the word "file".

The operating system has devices of various kinds. All of the various devices are unified using a common abstraction that we call the file system. All of a computer's devices appear as OS files of one kind or another. Some things which aren't physical devices also appear as files. Files are the plumbing that move data around our information infrastructure.

Additionally, Python defines file objects. These file objects are the fixtures that give our Python program access to OS files.

Python File and OS File

How Files Work. When your program evaluates a method function of a Python file object, Python transforms this into an operation on the underlying OS file. An OS file operation becomes an operation on one of the various kinds of devices attached to our computer. Or, a OS file operation can become a network operation that reaches through the Internet to access data from remote computers. The two layers of abstraction mean that one Python program can do a wide variety of things on a wide variety of devices.

Python File Objects

In Python, we create a file object to work with files in the file system. In addition to files in the

OS's file system, Python recognizes a spectrum of file-like objects, including abstractions for network interfaces called pipes and sockets and even some kind of in-memory buffers.

Unlike sequences, sets and mappings, there are no Python literals for file objects. Lacking literals, we create a file object using the file() or open() factory function. We provide two pieces of information to this function. We can provide a third, optional, piece of information that may improve the performance of our program.

The name of the file. The operating system will interpret this name using its "working directory" rules. If the name starts with / (or device:\) it's an absolute name. Otherwise, it's a relative name; the current working directory plus this name identifies the file.

Python can translate standard paths (using /) to Windows-specific paths. This saves us from having to really understand the differences. We can name all of our files using /, and avoid the messy details.

We can, if we want, use raw strings to specify Windows path names using the \ character.

The access mode for the file. This is some combination of read, write and append. The mode can also include instructions for interpreting the bytes as characters.

Optionally, we can include the buffering for the file. Generally, we omit this. If the buffering argument is given, 0 means each byte is transferred as it is read or written. A value of 1 means the data is buffered a line at a time, suitable for reading from a console, or writing to an error log. Larger numbers specify the buffer size: numbers over 4,096 may speed up your program.

Once we create the file object, we can do operations to read characters from the file or write characters to the file. We can read individual characters or whole lines. Similarly, we can write individual characters or whole lines.

When Python reads a file as a sequence of lines, each line will become a separate string. The '\n' character is preserved at the end of the string. This extra character can be removed from the string using the rstrip() method function.

A file object (like a sequence) can create an iterator which will yield the individual lines of the file. You can, consequently, use the file object in a for statement. This makes reading text files very simple.

When the work is finished, we also need to use the file's close() method. This empties the in-memory buffers and releases the connection with the operating system file. In the case of a socket connection, this will release all of the resources used to assure that data travels through the Internet successfully.

The File and Open Functions

Here's the formal definition of the file() and open() factory functions. These functions create Python file objects and connect them to the appropriate operating system resources.

open(filename, mode[, buffering]) → file

The filename is the name of the file. This is simply given to the operating system. The OS expects eitther absolute or relative paths; the operating system folds in the current working directory to relative paths.

The mode is covered in detail below. In can be 'r', 'w' or 'a' for reading (default), writing or appending. If the file doesn't exist when opened for writing or appending, it will be created. If a file existed when opened for writing, it will be truncated and overwritten. Add a 'b' to the mode for binary files. Add a '+' to the mode to allow simultaneous reading and writing.

If the buffering argument is given, 0 means unbuffered, 1 means line buffered, and larger numbers specify the buffer size.

file(filename, mode[, buffering]) → file
This is another name for the open() function. It parallels other factory functions like int() and dict().

Python expects the POSIX standard punctuation of / to separate elements of the filename path for all operating systems. If necessary, Python will translate these standard name strings to the Windows punctuation of \. Using standardized punctuation makes your program portable to all operating systems. The os.path module has functions for creating valid names in a way that works on all operating systems.

Tip Constructing File Names
When using Windows-specific punctuation for filenames, you'll have problems because Python interprets the \ as an escape character. To create a string with a Windows filename, you'll either need to use \ in the string, or use an r" " string literal. For example, you can use any of the following:
r"E:\writing\technical\pythonbook\python.html"
or
"E:\\writing\\technical\\pythonbook\\python.html".

Note that you can often use "E:/writing/technical/pythonbook/python.html". This uses the POSIX standard punctuation for files paths, /, and is the most portable. Python generally translates standard file names to Windows file names for you.

Generally, you should either use standard names (using /) or use the os.path module to construct filenames. This module eliminates the need to use any specific punctuation. The os.path.join() function makes properly punctuated filenames from sequences of strings

The Mode String. The mode string specifies how the OS file will be accessed by your program. There are four separate issues addressed by the mode string: opening, bytes, newlines and operations.

Opening. For the opening part of the mode string, there are three alternatives:

r: Open for reading. Start at the beginning of the OS file. If the OS file does not exist, raise an IOError exception. This is the default.

w: Open for writing. Start at he beginning of the OS file. If the OS file does not exist, create the OS file.

a: Open for appending. Start at the end of the OS file. If the OS file does not exist, create the OS file.

Bytes or Characters. For the byte handling part of the mode string, there are two alternatives:

b: The OS file is a sequence of bytes; do not interpret the file as a sequence of characters. This is suitable for .csv files as well as images, movies, sound samples, etc.

The default, if b is not included, is to interpret the file is a sequence of ordinary characters. The

Python file object will be an iterator that yields each individual line from the OS file as a separate string. Translations from various encoding schemes like UTF-8 and UTF-16 will be handled automatically.

Universal Newlines. The newline part of the mode string has two alternatives:

U: Universal newline interpretation. The first instance of \n, \r\n (or \r) will define the newline character(s). Any of these three newline sequences will be silently translated to the standard '\n' character. The \r\n is a Windows feature.

The default, if U is not included, is to only handle this operating system's standard newline character(s).

Mixed Operations. For the additional operations part of the mode string, there are two alternatives:

+: Allow both read and write operations to the OS file.

The default, if + is not included, is to allow only limited operations: only reads for files opened with "r"; only writes for OS files opened with "w" or "a".

Typical combinations include the following:

"r" to read text files.

"rb" to read binary files. A .csv file, for example, is often processed in binary mode.

"w+" to create new text file for reading and writing.

The following examples create Python file objects for further processing:

```
dataSource= open( "name_addr.csv", "rb" )
newPage= open( "addressbook.html", "w" )
theErrors= open( "/usr/local/log/error.log", "a" )
```

dataSource:

This example opens the existing file name_addr.csv in the current working directory for reading. The variable dataSource identifies this file object, and we can use this variable for reading strings from this file.

This file is opened in binary mode.

newPage:

This example creates a new file addressbook.html (or it will truncate this file if it exists). The file will be in the current working directory. The variable newPage identifies the file object. We can then use this variable to write strings to the file.

theErrors:

This example appends to the file error.log (or creates a new file, if the file doesn't exist). The file has the directory path /usr/local/log/. Since this is an absolute name, it doesn't depend on the current working directory.

Buffering files is typically left as a default, specifying nothing. However, for some situations, adjusting the buffering can improve performance. Error logs, for instance, are often unbuffered, so the data is available immediately. Large input files may be opened with large buffer numbers to encourage the operating system to optimize input operations by reading a few large chunks of data from the device instead of a large number of smaller chunks.

Tip Debugging Files
There are a number of things that can go wrong in attempting to create a file object.

If the file name is invalid, you will get operating system errors. Usually they will look like this:

```
Traceback (most recent call last):
  File "<stdin>", line 1, in <module>
IOError: [Errno 2] No such file or directory: 'wakawaka'
```

It is very important to get the file's path completely correct. You'll notice that each time you start IDLE, it thinks the current working directory is something like C:\Python26. You're probably doing your work in a different default directory.

When you open a module file in IDLE, you'll notice that IDLE changes the current working directory is the directory that contains your module. If you have your .py files and your data files all in one directory, you'll find that things work out well.

The next most common error is to have the wrong permissions. This usually means trying to writing to a file you don't own, or attempting to create a file in a directory where you don't have write permission. If you are using a server, or a computer owned by a corporation, this may require some work with your system administrators to sort out what you want to do and how you can accomplish it without compromising security.

The [Errno 2] note in the error message is a reference to the internal operating system error numbers. There are over 100 of these error numbers, all collected into the module named errno. There are a lot of different things that can go wrong, many of which are very, very obscure situations.

Methods We Use on File Objects

The Python file object is our view of the underlying operating system file. The OS file, in turn, gives us access to a specific device.

The Python file object has a number of operations that transform the file object, read from or write to the OS file, or access information about the file object.

Reading. The following read methods get data from the OS file. These operations may also change the Python file object's internal status and buffers. For example, at end-of-file, the internal status of the file object will be changed. Most importantly, these methods have the very visible effect of consuming data from the OS file.

file.read(size) → string
Read as many as size characters from file f as a single, large string. If size is negative or omitted, the rest of the file is read into a single string.

from __future__ import print_function
dataSource= open("name_addr.csv", "r")

```
theData= dataSource.read()
for n in theData.splitlines():
    print(n)
dataSource.close()
```

file.readline(size) → string

Read the next line or as many as size characters from file f; an incomplete line can be read. If size is negative or omitted, the next complete line is read. If a complete line is read, it includes the trailing newline character. If the file is at the end, f. readline() returns a zero length string. If the file has a blank line, this will be a string of length 1, just the newline character.

```
from __future__ import print_function
dataSource= file( "name_addr.csv", "r" )
n= dataSource.readline()
while len(n) > 0:
    print(n.rstrip())
    n= dataSource.readline()
dataSource.close()
```

file.readlines(hint)

Read the next lines or as many lines from the next hint characters from file f. The hint size may be rounded up to match an internal buffer size. If hint is negative or omitted, the rest of the file is read. All lines will include the trailing newline character. If the file is at the end, f. readlines() returns a zero length list.

When we simply reference a file object in a for statement, this is the function that's used for iteration over the file.

```
dataSource= file( "name_addr.csv", "r" )
for n in dataSource:
    print(n.rstrip())
dataSource.close()
```

Writing. The following methods send data to the OS file. These operations may also change the Python file object's internal status and buffers.

Most importantly, these methods have the very visible effect of producing data to the OS file.

file.flush()
Flush all accumulated data from the internal buffers of file f to the device or interface. If a file is buffered, this can help to force writing of a buffer that is less than completely full. This is appropriate for log files, prompts written to sys.stdout and error messages.

file.truncate(size)
Truncate file f. If size is not given, the file is truncated at the current position. If size is given, the file will be truncated at or before size. This function is not available on all platforms.

file.write(string)
Write the given string to file f. Buffering may mean that the string does not appear on a console until a close() or flush() operation is used.

```
newPage= file( "addressbook.html", "w" )
newPage.write( "<html>\n<head><title>Hello World</title></head>\n<body>\n" )
newPage.write( "<p>Hello World</p>\n" )
newPage.write( "<\body>\n</html>\n" )
newPage.close()
```

file.writelines(list)

Write the list of strings to file f. Buffering may mean that the strings do not appear on any console until a close() or flush() operation is used.

```
newPage= file( "addressbook.html", "w" )
newPage.writelines( [ "<html>\n", "<head><title>Hello World</title></head>\n", "<body>\n" ] )
newPage.writelines( ["<p>Hello World</p>\n" ] )
newPage.writelines( [ "<\body>\n", "</html>\n" ] )
newPage.close()
```

Accessors. The following file accessors provide information about the file object.

file.tell() → integer

Return the position from which file f will be processed. This is a partner to the seek() method; any position returned by the tell() method can be used as an argument to the seek() method to restore the file to that position.

file.fileno() → integer

Return the internal file descriptor (fd) number used by the OS library when working with file f. A number of modules provide access to these low-level libraries for advanced operations on devices and files.

file.isatty() → boolean

Return True if file f is connected to an OS file that is a console or keyboard.

file.closed() → boolean

This attribute of file f is True if the file is closed.

file.mode() → string

This attribute is the mode argument to the file() function that was used to create the file object.

file.name

This attribute of file f is the filename argument to the file() function that was used to create the file object.

Transfomers. The following file transforms change the file object itself. This includes closing it (and releasing all OS resources) or change the position at which reading or writing happens.

file.close()

Close file f. The closed flag is set. Any further operations (except a redundant close) raise an IOError exception.

file.seek(offset[, whence])
Change the position from which file f will be processed. There are three values for whence which determine the direction of the move.

If whence is 0 (the default), move to the absolute position given by offset. f.seek(0) will rewind file f.

If whence is 1, move relative to the current position by offset bytes. If offset is negative, move backwards; otherwise move forward.

If whence is 2, move relative to the end of file. f.seek(0,2) will advance file f to the end.

File Statements: Reading and Writing (but no Arithmetic)
A file object (like a sequence) can create an iterator which will yield the individual lines of the

file. We looked at how sequences work with the for statement in Looping Back : Iterators, the for statement and Generators. Here, we'll use the file object in a for statement to read all of the lines.

Additionally, the print statement can make use of a file other than standard output as a destination for the printed characters. This will change with Python 3.0, so we won't emphasize this.

Opening and Reading From a File. Let's say we have the following file. If you use an email service like HotMail, Yahoo! or Google, you can download an address book in Comma-Separated Values (CSV) format that will look similar to this file. Yahoo!'s format will have many more columns than this example.

name_addr.csv

"First","Middle","Last","Nickname","Email","Category"

"Moe","","Howard","Moe","moe@3stooges.com","actor"
"Jerome","Lester","Howard","Curly","curly@3stooges.com","actor"
"Larry","","Fine","Larry","larry@3stooges.com","musician"
"Jerome","","Besser","Joe","joe@3stooges.com","actor"
"Joe","","DeRita","CurlyJoe","curlyjoe@3stooges.com","actor"
"Shemp","","Howard","Shemp","shemp@3stooges.com","actor"

Here's a quick example that shows one way to read this file using the file's iterator. This isn't the best way, that will have to wait for The csv Module.

1
2
3
4

```
dataSource = file( "name_addr.csv", "r" )
for addr in dataSource:
    print(addr)
dataSource.close()
```

We create a Python file object for the name_addr.csv in the current working directory in read mode. We call this object dataSource.

The for statement creates an iterator for this file; the iterator will yield each individual line from the file.

We can print each line.

We close the file when we're done. This releases any operating system resources that our program tied up while it was running.

A More Complete Reader. Here's a program that reads this file and reformats the individual records. It prints the results to standard output. This approach to reading CSV files isn't very good. In the next chapter, we'll look at the csv module that handles some of the additional details required for a really reliable program.

nameaddr.py

1
2
3
4
5
6
7
8
9
10

```
#!/usr/bin/env python
"""Read the name_addr.csv file."""
dataSource = file( "name_addr.csv", "r" )
for addr in dataSource:
    # split the string on the ,'s
    quotes= addr.split(",")
    # strip the ""s from each field
    fields= [ f.strip('"') for f in quotes ]
```

```
    print( fields[0], fields[1], fields[2], fields[4] )
dataSource.close()
```

We open the file name_addr.csv in our current working directory. The variable dataSource is our Python file object.

The for statement gets an iterator from the file. It can then use the iterator, which yields the individual lines of the file. Each line is a long string. The fields are surrounded by "s and are separated by ,s.

We use the split() function to break the string up using the ,s. This particular process won't work if there are ,s inside the quoted fields. We'll look at the csv module to see how to do this better.

We use the strip() function to remove the "s from each field. Notice that we used a list comprehension to map from a list of fields wrapped in "s to a list of fields that are not wrapped in "s.

Seeing Output with print. The print() function does two things. When we introduced print() back in Seeing Results : The print Statement, we hustled past both of these things because they were really quite advanced concepts.

We covered strings in Sequences of Characters : str and Unicode. We're covering files in this chapter. Now we can open up the hood and look closely at the print() function.

The print() function evaluates all of its expressions and converts them to strings. In effect, it calls the str() built-in function for each argument value.

The print() function writes these strings, separated by a separator character, sep. The default separator is a space, ' '.

The print() function also writes an end character, end. The default end is the newline character, '\n'.

The print() function has one more feature which can be very helpful to us. We can provide a file parameter to redirect the output to a particular file.

We can use this to write lines to sys.stderr.

```
1
2
3
4
5
from __future__ import print_function
import sys
print("normal output")
print("Red Alert!", file=sys.stderr)
print("still normal output", file=sys.stdout)
```

We enable the print function.

We import the sys module.

We write a message to standard output using the undecorated print statement.

We use the file parameter to write to sys.stderr.

We also use the:varname:file parameter to write to sys.stdout.

When you run this in IDLE, you'll notice that the error messages display in red, while the standard output displays in blue.

Print Command. Here is the syntax for an extension to the print statement.

print >> file [, expression , ...]

The >> is an essential part of this peculiar syntax. This is an odd special case punctuation that doesn't appear elsewhere in the Python language. It's called the "chevron print".

Important Python 3

This chevron print syntax will go away in Python 3. Instead of a print statement with a bunch of special cases, we'll use the print() function.

Opening A File and Printing. This example shows how we open a file in the local directory and write data to that file. In this example, we'll create an HTML file named addressbook.html. We'll write some content to this file. We can then open this file with FireFox or Internet Explorer and see the resulting web page.

addrpage.py

1
2
3
4
5
6
7
8
9
10
11

```python
#!/usr/bin/env python
"""Write the addressbook.html page."""
from __future__ import print_function
new_page = open( "addressbook.html", "w" )
print('<html>', new_page)
print(' <head>'
    '<meta http-equiv="content-type" content="text/html; charset=us-ascii">'
    '<title>addressbook</title></head>',
    file=new_page)
print(' <body><p>Hello world</p></body>', file=new_page )
print('</html>', file=new_page)
new_page.close()
```

Basic File Exercises

Device Structures.

Some disk devices are organized into cylinders and tracks instead of blocks. A disk may have a number of parallel platters; a cylinder is the stack of tracks across the platters available without moving the read-write head. A track is the data on one circular section of a single disk platter. What advantages does this have? What (if any) complexity could this lead to? How does an application program specify the tracks and sectors to be used?

Some disk devices are described as a simple sequence of blocks, in no particular order. Each block has a unique numeric identifier. What advantages could this have?

Some disk devices can be partitioned. What (if any) relevance does this have to file processing?

Skip The Header Record.

Our name_addr.csv file has a header record. We can skip this record by getting the iterator and advancing to the next item.

Write a variation on nameaddr.py which uses the iter() to get the iterator for the dataSource file. Assign this iterator object to dataSrcIter. If you replace the file, dataSource, with the iterator, dataSrcIter, how does the processing change? What is the value returned by dataSrcIter.next() before the for statement? How does adding this change the processing of the for statement?

Combine The Two Examples.

Our two examples, addrpage.py and name_addr.py are really two halves of a single program. One program reads the names and address, the other program writes an HTML file. We can combine these two programs to reformat a CSV source file into a resulting HTML page.

The name and addresses could be formatted in a web page that looks like the following:

```html
<html>
<head><title>Address Book</title></head>
<body>
<table>
<tr><td>last name</td><td>first name</td><td>email address</td></tr>
<tr><td>last name</td><td>first name</td><td>email address</td></tr>
<tr><td>last name</td><td>first name</td><td>email address</td></tr>
...
</table>
</body>
</html>
```

Each of our input fields becomes an output field sandwiched in between <td> and </td>. In this case, we uses phrases like last name, first name and email address to show where real data would be inserted. The other HTML elements like <table> have to be printed as they're shown in this example.

Your final program should open two files: name_addr.csv and addressbook.html. Your program should write the initial HTML material (up to the first <tr>) to the output file. It should then read the CSV records, writing a complete address line between <tr> to </tr>. After it finishes reading and writing names and addresses, it has to write the last of the HTML file, from </table> to </html>.

CHAPTER 6

DISCOVER VARIABLES, STRINGS, INTEGERS, AND MORE TO DESIGN CONVERSATIONAL PROGRAMS

Before we start to write the program, we need to generate a token for our bot. The token is needed to access the Telegram API, and install the necessary dependencies.

1. Create a new bot in BotFather

If you want to make a bot in Telegram, you have to "register" your bot first before using it. When we "register" our bot, we will get the token to access the Telegram API.

Go to the BotFather (if you open it in desktop, make sure you have the Telegram app), then create new bot by sending the /newbot command. Follow the steps until you get the username and token for your bot. You can go to your bot by accessing this URL: https://telegram.me/YOUR_BOT_USERNAME and your token should looks like this.

704418931:AAEtcZ*************

2. Install the library

Since we are going to use a library for this tutorial, install it using this command.

pip3 install python-telegram-bot

If the library is successfully installed, then we are good to go.

Write the program

Let's make our first bot. This bot should return a dog image when we send the /bop command. To be able to do this, we can use the public API from RandomDog to help us generate random dog images.

The workflow of our bot is as simple as this:

access the API -> get the image URL -> send the image

1. Import the libraries

First, import all the libraries we need.

```
from telegram.ext import Updater, CommandHandler
import requests
import re
```

2. Access the API and get the image URL

Let's create a function to get the URL. Using the requests library, we can access the API and get the json data.

```
contents = requests.get('https://random.dog/woof.json').json()
```
You can check the json data by accessing that URL: https://random.dog/woof.json in your browser. You will see something like this on your screen:

```
{"url":"https://random.dog/*****.JPG"}
```
Get the image URL since we need that parameter to be able to send the image.

```
image_url = contents['url']
```
Wrap this code into a function called get_url() .

```
def get_url():
    contents = requests.get('https://random.dog/woof.json').json()
    url = contents['url']
    return url
```

3. Send the image

To send a message/image we need two parameters, the image URL and the recipient's ID—this can be group ID or user ID.

We can get the image URL by calling our get_url() function.

```
url = get_url()
```
Get the recipient's ID using this code:

```
chat_id = update.message.chat_id
```
After we get the image URL and the recipient's ID, it's time to send the message, which is an image.

```
bot.send_photo(chat_id=chat_id, photo=url)
```
Wrap that code in a function called bop , and make sure your code looks like this:

```
def bop(bot, update):
    url = get_url()
```

```
    chat_id = update.message.chat_id
    bot.send_photo(chat_id=chat_id, photo=url)
```

4. Main program

Lastly, create another function called main to run our program. Don't forget to change YOUR_TOKEN with the token that we generated earlier in this tutorial.

```
def main():
    updater = Updater('YOUR_TOKEN')
    dp = updater.dispatcher
    dp.add_handler(CommandHandler('bop',bop))
    updater.start_polling()
    updater.idle()
if __name__ == '__main__':
    main()
```

At the end your code should look like this:

```
from telegram.ext import Updater, InlineQueryHandler, CommandHandler
import requests
```

```python
import re
def get_url():
    contents = requests.get('https://random.dog/woof.json').json()
    url = contents['url']
    return url
def bop(bot, update):
    url = get_url()
    chat_id = update.message.chat_id
    bot.send_photo(chat_id=chat_id, photo=url)
def main():
    updater = Updater('YOUR_TOKEN')
    dp = updater.dispatcher
    dp.add_handler(CommandHandler('bop',bop))
    updater.start_polling()
    updater.idle()
if __name__ == '__main__':
    main()
```

5. Run the program

Awesome! You finished your first program. Now let's check if it works. Save the file, name it main.py , then run it using this command.

python3 main.py

Go to your telegram bot by accessing this URL: https://telegram.me/YOUR_BOT_USERNAME. Send the /bop command. If everything runs perfectly the bot will reply with a random dog image. Cute right?

Handling errors

Great! Now you have a bot that will send you a cute dog image whenever you want.

There is more! The RandomDog API not only generates images, but also videos and GIFs. If we access the API and we get a video or GIF, there is an error and the bot won't send it to you.

Let's fix this so the bot will only send a message with an image attachment. If we get a video or GIF then we will call the API again until we get an image.

1. Match the file extension using regex

We are going to use a regex to solve this problem.

To distinguish an image from video or GIF, we can take a look at the file extension. We only need the last part of our URL.

https://random.dog/*****.JPG

We need to define, first, what file extensions are allowed in our program.

allowed_extension = ['jpg','jpeg','png']

Then use the regex to extract the file extension from the URL.

file_extension = re.search("([^.]*)$",url).group(1).lower()

Using that code, make a function called get_image_url() to iterate the URL until we get the file extension that we want (jpg,jpeg,png).

```python
def get_image_url():
    allowed_extension = ['jpg','jpeg','png']
    file_extension = ''
    while file_extension not in allowed_extension:
        url = get_url()
        file_extension = re.search("([^.]*)$",url).group(1).lower()
    return url
```

2. Modify your code

Great! Now for the last part, replace the url = get_url() line in the bop() function with url = get_image_url() , and your code should look like this:

```python
from telegram.ext import Updater, InlineQueryHandler, CommandHandler
import requests
import re
def get_url():
    contents = requests.get('https://random.dog/woof.json').json()
    url = contents['url']
    return url
def get_image_url():
    allowed_extension = ['jpg','jpeg','png']
    file_extension = ''
    while file_extension not in allowed_extension:
        url = get_url()
        file_extension = re.search("([^.]*)$",url).group(1).lower()
    return url
def bop(bot, update):
    url = get_image_url()
    chat_id = update.message.chat_id
    bot.send_photo(chat_id=chat_id, photo=url)
```

```python
def main():
    updater = Updater('YOUR_TOKEN')
    dp = updater.dispatcher
    dp.add_handler(CommandHandler('bop',bop))
    updater.start_polling()
    updater.idle()
if __name__ == '__main__':
    main().
```

CHAPTER 7

UNDERSTAND "GRAPHICAL USER INTERFACES" AND CREATE YOUR OWN ARCADE GAMES AND APPS.

Arcade, like many other packages, is available via PyPi, which means you can install Arcade using the pip command (or the pipenv command). If you already have Python installed, you can likely just open up a command prompt on Windows and type:

pip install arcade

Or on MacOS and Linux type:

pip3 install arcade

For more detailed installation instructions, you can refer to the Arcade installation documentation.

Simple drawing

You can open a window and create simple drawings with just a few lines of code.

The script below shows how you can use Arcade's drawing commands to do this. Note that you don't need to know how to use classes or even define functions. Programming with quick visual feedback is great for anyone who wants to start learning to program.

import arcade

```python
# Set constants for the screen size
SCREEN_WIDTH = 600
SCREEN_HEIGHT = 600

# Open the window. Set the window title and dimensions (width and height)
arcade.open_window(SCREEN_WIDTH, SCREEN_HEIGHT, "Drawing Example")

# Set the background color to white.
# For a list of named colors see:
# http://arcade.academy/arcade.color.html
# Colors can also be specified in (red, green, blue) format and
# (red, green, blue, alpha) format.
arcade.set_background_color(arcade.color.WHITE)

# Start the render process. This must be done before any drawing commands.
arcade.start_render()
```

```python
# Draw the face
x = 300
y = 300
radius = 200
arcade.draw_circle_filled(x, y, radius, arcade.color.YELLOW)

# Draw the right eye
x = 370
y = 350
radius = 20
arcade.draw_circle_filled(x, y, radius, arcade.color.BLACK)

# Draw the left eye
x = 230
y = 350
radius = 20
arcade.draw_circle_filled(x, y, radius, arcade.color.BLACK)
```

```
# Draw the smile
x = 300
y = 280
width = 120
height = 100
start_angle = 190
end_angle = 350
arcade.draw_arc_outline(x, y, width, height,
arcade.color.BLACK, start_angle, end_angle, 10)

# Finish drawing and display the result
arcade.finish_render()

# Keep the window open until the user hits the 'close' button
arcade.run()
```

Using functions

Of course, writing code in the global context isn't good form. Thankfully improving your program by using functions is easy. Here we can see an example of a drawing a pine tree at a specific (x, y) location using a function:

```
def draw_pine_tree(x, y):
    """ This function draws a pine tree at the specified location. """

    # Draw the triangle on top of the trunk.
    # We need three x, y points for the triangle.
    arcade.draw_triangle_filled(x + 40, y,      # Point 1
                                x, y - 100,     # Point 2
                                x + 80, y - 100, # Point 3
                                arcade.color.DARK_GREEN)

    # Draw the trunk
    arcade.draw_lrtb_rectangle_filled(x + 30, x + 50, y - 100, y - 140,
                                      arcade.color.DARK_BROWN)
```

The more experienced programmer will know that modern graphics programs first load drawing information onto the graphics card, and then ask the graphics card to draw it later as a batch. Arcade supports this as well. Drawing 10,000 rectangles individually takes about 0.800 seconds. Drawing them as a batch takes less that 0.001 seconds.

The Window class

Larger programs will typically derive from the Window class, or use decorators. This allows a programmer to write code to handle drawing, updating, and handling input from the user. A template for a starting a Window-based program is below.

```python
import arcade

SCREEN_WIDTH = 800
SCREEN_HEIGHT = 600


class MyGame(arcade.Window):
    """ Main application class. """

    def __init__(self, width, height):
        super().__init__(width, height)


arcade.set_background_color(arcade.color.AMAZON)

    def setup(self):
        # Set up your game here
        pass

    def on_draw(self):
```

```python
        """ Render the screen. """
        arcade.start_render()
        # Your drawing code goes here

    def update(self, delta_time):
        """ All the logic to move, and the game logic
goes here. """
        pass


def main():
    game = MyGame(SCREEN_WIDTH, SCREEN_HEIGHT)
    game.setup()
    arcade.run()


if __name__ == "__main__":
    main()
```

The Window class has several methods that your programs can override to provide functionality to the program. Here are some of the most commonly used ones:

on_draw: All the code to draw the screen goes here.

update: All the code to move your items and perform game logic goes here. This is called about 60 times per second.

on_key_press: Handle events when a key is pressed, such as giving a player a speed.

on_key_release: Handle when a key is released, here you might stop a player from moving.

on_mouse_motion: This is called every time the mouse moves.

on_mouse_press: Called when a mouse button is pressed.

set_viewport: This function is used in scrolling games, when you have a world much larger than what can be seen on one screen. Calling set_viewport allows a programmer to set what part of that world is currently visible.

Sprites

Sprites are an easy way to create a 2D bitmapped object in Arcade. Arcade has methods that make it easy to draw, move, and animate sprites. You can also easily use sprites to detect collisions between objects.

Creating a sprite

Creating an instance of Arcade's Sprite class out of a graphic is easy. A programmer only needs the file name of an image to base the sprite off of, and optionally a number to scale the image up or down. For example:

SPRITE_SCALING_COIN = 0.2

coin = arcade.Sprite("coin_01.png", SPRITE_SCALING_COIN)

This code will create a sprite using the image stored in coin_01.png. The image will be scaled down to 20% of its original height and width.

Sprite lists

Sprites are normally organized into lists. These lists make it easier to manage the sprites. Sprites in a list will use OpenGL to batch-draw the sprites as a group. The code below sets up a game with a player, and a bunch of coins for the player to collect. We use two lists, one for the player and one for the coins.

```
def setup(self):
    """ Set up the game and initialize the variables.
"""

    # Create the sprite lists
    self.player_list = arcade.SpriteList()
    self.coin_list = arcade.SpriteList()
```

```python
        # Score
        self.score = 0

        # Set up the player
        # Character image from kenney.nl
        self.player_sprite = arcade.Sprite("images/character.png", SPRITE_SCALING_PLAYER)
        self.player_sprite.center_x = 50 # Starting position
        self.player_sprite.center_y = 50
        self.player_list.append(self.player_sprite)

        # Create the coins
        for i in range(COIN_COUNT):

            # Create the coin instance
            # Coin image from kenney.nl
            coin = arcade.Sprite("images/coin_01.png", SPRITE_SCALING_COIN)
```

```
    # Position the coin
    coin.center_x = random.randrange(SCREEN_WIDTH)
    coin.center_y = random.randrange(SCREEN_HEIGHT)

    # Add the coin to the lists
    self.coin_list.append(coin)
```

We can easily draw all the coins in the coin lists:

```
def on_draw(self):
    """ Draw everything """
    arcade.start_render()
    self.coin_list.draw()
    self.player_list.draw()
```

Detecting sprite collisions

The function check_for_collision_with_list allows us to see if a sprite runs into another sprite in a list. We can use this to see all the coins the player sprite is in contact with. Using a simple for loop, we can get rid of the coin from the game and increase our score.

```
def update(self, delta_time):
    # Generate a list of all coin sprites that collided with the player.
    coins_hit_list = arcade.check_for_collision_with_list(self.player_sprite, self.coin_list)

    # Loop through each colliding sprite, remove it, and add to the score.
    for coin in coins_hit_list:
        coin.kill()
        self.score += 1
```

For the full example, see collect_coins.py.

Game physics

Many games include some kind of physics. The simplest are top-down programs that prevent the player from walking through walls. Platformers add more complexity with gravity and platforms that move. Some games use a full 2D physics engine with mass, friction, springs, and more.

For simple top-down based games, an Arcade program needs a list of walls that the player (or anything else) can't move through. I usually call this wall_list. Then a physics engine is created in the Window class's setup code with:

self.physics_engine = arcade.PhysicsEngineSimple(self.player_sprite, self.wall_list)

The player_sprite is given a movement vector with its two attributes change_x and change_y. A simple example of doing this would be to have the player move with the keyboard. For example, this might be in the custom child of the Window class:

```python
MOVEMENT_SPEED = 5

def on_key_press(self, key, modifiers):
    """Called whenever a key is pressed. """

    if key == arcade.key.UP:
        self.player_sprite.change_y = MOVEMENT_SPEED
    elif key == arcade.key.DOWN:
        self.player_sprite.change_y = -MOVEMENT_SPEED
    elif key == arcade.key.LEFT:
        self.player_sprite.change_x = -MOVEMENT_SPEED
    elif key == arcade.key.RIGHT:
        self.player_sprite.change_x = MOVEMENT_SPEED

def on_key_release(self, key, modifiers):
    """Called when the user releases a key. """
```

```
    if key == arcade.key.UP or key ==
arcade.key.DOWN:
        self.player_sprite.change_y = 0
    elif key == arcade.key.LEFT or key ==
arcade.key.RIGHT:
        self.player_sprite.change_x = 0
```

Although that code sets the player's speed, it doesn't move the player. In the update method of the Window class, calling physics_engine.update() will move the player, but not through walls.

```
def update(self, delta_time):
    """ Movement and game logic """

    self.physics_engine.update()
```

Moving to a side view platformer is rather easy. A programmer just needs to switch the physics engine to PhysicsEnginePlatformer and add in the gravity constant.

```
self.physics_engine =
arcade.PhysicsEnginePlatformer(self.player_sprite,
                               self.wall_list,
                               gravity_constant=GRAVITY)
```

You can use a program like Tiled to lay the tiles/blocks that make up your level.

For an example, see sprite_tiled_map.py.

For full 2D physics you can integrate the PyMunk library.

Learn by example

One of the best ways to learn is by example. The Arcade library has a long list of example programs that a person can draw on to create games. These examples each show a game concept that students have asked for in my classes or online over the years.

Running any of these demos is easy once Arcade has been installed. Each of the samples has a comment at the beginning of the program with a command you can type on the command-line to run the sample, for example:

python -m arcade.examples.sprite_moving_platforms.

CHAPTER 8

HOW BENEFICIAL IS DJANGO FOR THE EXISTING PYTHON DEVELOPERS

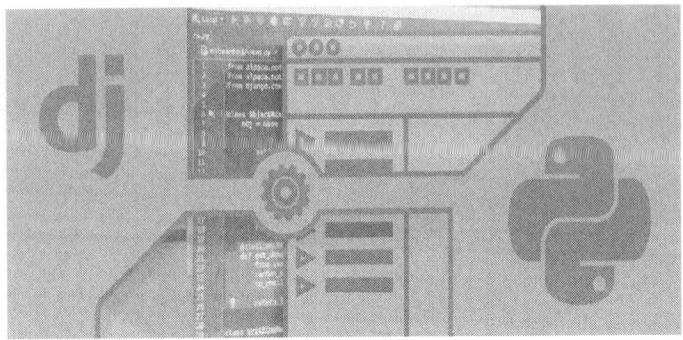

As a powerful server side scripting language, Python makes it easier for developers to build high-performing websites rapidly. The object-oriented programming language supports modules and packages. So the developers can divide the code into different modules, and reuse these modules across different projects. They can further reduce overall development time and efforts significantly by using a Python web framework.

As highlighted by several surveys, existing Python developers across the world prefer Django to other popular Python web frameworks like TurboGears, Falcon, Pyramid, web2py and web.py. Along with being a high-level web framework, Django is also flexible and extensible, and comes with features that help developers to create customized internet applications. There are also a number of reasons why Django is hugely popular among both beginners and existing Python programmers.

What Makes Django Popular Among Existing Python Programmers?

SHORTER AND CLEANER CODE

The existing Python programmers understand the long-term benefits of a shorter and cleaner code base. As Python enables those to express common concepts with less code, they can always avoid creating longer code. At the same time, Django supports model-view-controller (MVC) pattern. The pattern makes it easier for programmers to organize their code efficiently by keeping the business logic, user interface and application data separate. The combination of Python and Django helps experienced developers to create readable, shorter and cleaner code.

OPTIONS TO CUSTOMIZE WEB APPLICATIONS

Nowadays each business wants its website to deliver distinct and rich user experience. Python developers look for options to customize pieces of websites without putting any extra time and effort. As a flexible web framework, Django enables them to customize different pieces of a website. Instead of using pre-built web applications, the programmers are required to focus only on customizing pieces of the website according to client's specific requirements. The focus enables them to create applications that deliver relevant content or information according to the specific needs of user.

BUILT-IN TOOLS FOR ACCOMPLISHING COMMON TASKS

Django is being updated regularly with new features and built-in tools. It includes a variety of built-in tools that help users to accomplish common web development tasks without writing lengthy code. These built-in tools help programmers to reduce the amount of time required for developing large websites.

A VARIETY OF PACKAGES

The existing Python programmers further boost performance of their web application using Django packages. The Django packages include reusable tools, apps, and sites. Many developers frequently use apps like Django Extensions, Django Celery, Django Rest Framework and South. They also effectuate development of ecommerce websites by using django SHOP, django-oscar, Satchmo, satchless or Cartridge. They also have option to choose from a variety of reusable tools, apps and sites according to the nature and needs of the web application. These packages make it easier for them to boost the website's performance without writing extra code.

OBJECT-RELATIONAL MAPPER (ORM)

The choice of database differs from one client to another. The experienced Python developers prefer using object-relational mapper to write database queries without using SQL. Django comes with an ORM that enables developers to manipulate database without writing lengthy SQL queries. The framework implements the ORM by default to allow programmers to describe the database layout as a Python class. At the same time, they also have option to use a Python API to access data in a more efficient way. As the API is generated on the fly, the developers are not required to generate any additional code. That is why; Django is used widely for development of data-driven websites.

HUMAN READABLE URLS

The beginners often ignore the significance of human readable URLs. But existing Python developers understand the benefits of human readable URLs for the web application. The website visitors can understand and remember the URL more easily. Also, the human readable URLs will make the web pages rank higher on search engine results pages. Django makes it easier for programmers to create simple, readable and easy-to-remember URLs for both website visitors and search engine bottoms.

DYNAMIC ADMIN INTERFACE

Each client wants a simple and dynamic admin interface to manage the application smoothly. Django is designed with features to generate a production-ready admin interface. The dynamic admin interface allows authenticate users to add, delete and change objects. Thus, it makes it easier for the business to edit or update the website content, without using any backend interface. The existing Python programmers take advantage of this feature to setup and run admin sites while developing the models.

OPTIMIZED SECURITY

Python scores over other popular web programming language in the category of security. The existing Python developers also avail the features of Django to optimize the security of Python web application. Unlike other web frameworks, Django often generates web pages dynamically, and sends the content to web browsers through templates. So the source code remains hidden from both the web browser and end users. As the source code is not directly exposed to the end users, the internet application gets comprehensive security cover. At the same time, the developers can also use Django to prevent cross-site scripting attacks, SQL injection and other security threats.

OPTION TO EXCHANGE IDEAS

Like other open source technologies, Django is also supported by a large and active community. So the existing Python web developer often avail assistance of the community to handle new issues. At the same time, they also exchange ideas and best practices with other members of the community on a regular basis. The exchange makes it easier for them to keep track of the latest trends in web development, along with understanding how to implement these trends without any hassle.

The existing Python programmers also upgrade to the latest version of Django to avail new features and enhancements, along with a number of bug fixes. Further, they can avail regular security updates for the most recent version of the web framework to protect the application from latest security threats. Many programmers even upgrade to the latest version of Django to keep their code base relevant and up to date.

CHAPTER 9

IMPORTANT PYTHON FRAMEWORKS

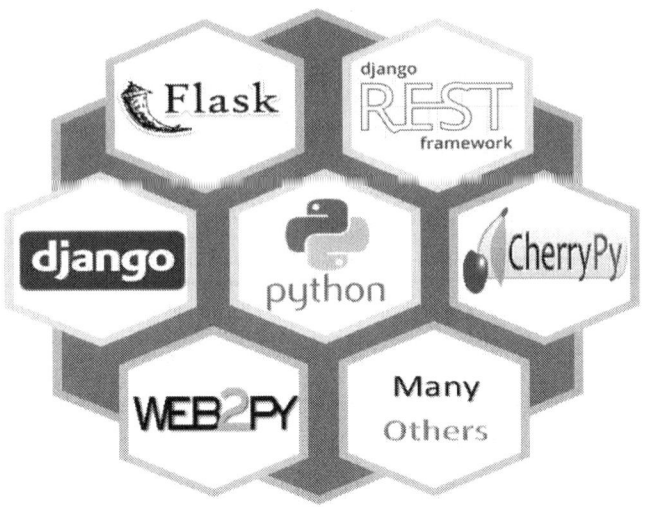

As a dynamic, general purpose and object-oriented programming language, Python is used widely by developers across the world for building a variety of software applications. Unlike other modern programming languages, Python enables programmers to express concept with less and readable code. The users also have an option to integrate Python with other popular programming languages and tools seamlessly. But it cannot be used directly for writing different types of software.

Often Python developers have to use a variety of frameworks and tools to build high quality software applications within a shorter amount of time. The resources provided by the Python frameworks help users to reduce the time and effort required for modern applications. They also have an option to choose from a number of frameworks according to the nature and requirements of individual projects. However, it is also important for the programmers to know some of the Python frameworks that will remain popular in the longer run.

10 Python Frameworks that will Remain Popular :

1) Kivy

As an open source Python library, Kivy makes it easier for programmers to build multi-touch user interfaces. It supports a number of popular platforms including Windows, Linux, OS X, iOS and Android. So the cross-platform framework enables users to create the app for multiple platforms using the same code base. It is also designed with features to take advantage of the native inputs, protocols and devices. Kivy further includes a fast graphic engine, while allowing users to choose from more than 20 extensible widgets.

2) Qt

The open source Python framework is written in C++. Qt enables developers to build connected applications and UIs that run on multiple operating systems and devices. The developers can further create cross-platform applications and UIs without making any changes to the code. Qt further scores over other frameworks due to its comprehensive library of APIs and tools. The programmers have option to use Qt either under the community license or the commercial license.

3) PyGUI

PyGUI is considered to be simpler than other Python frameworks. But it enables developers to create GUI API by taking advantage of the language features of Python. PyGUI currently supports Windows, OS X and Linux. So the developers can use it for creating lightweight GUI APIs that can be implemented on these three platforms. They can further document the API comprehensively without referring to the documentation of any third-party GUI library.

4) WxPython

The GUI toolkit for Python helps programmers to create applications with highly functional graphical user interfaces. As wxPython supports Windows, Linux and OS X, it becomes easier for developers to run the same program in multiple platforms without modifying the code. The users can write the programs in Python, while taking advantage of the 2D path drawing engine, standard dialogs, dockable windows and other features provided by the framework.

5) Django

Django is the most popular high-level web application development framework for Python. Despite being open source, Django provides a simple and rapid development environment for building a variety of websites and web applications rapidly. It further helps programmers to create web application without writing lengthy code. It further comes with features to prevent some of the common security mistakes made by the developers.

6) CherryPy

As a minimalist web framework, CherryPy enables programs to create websites and web applications just like writing other object-oriented Python programs. So it becomes easier for developers to build web applications without writing lengthy code. CherryPy further comes with a clean interface, while allowing developers to decide the right frontend utilities and data storage option. Despite being the oldest Python web application development framework in the market, CherryPy is still being used by programmers to create a variety of modern websites.

7) Flask

Flask is one of the micro web frameworks available for Python. Its core is simple and easy to use, but highly extensible. It also lacks many features provided by other web frameworks including database abstraction layer and form validations. Also, it does not allow users to add common functionality to the web application through third-party libraries. However, Flask enables programmers to create website rapidly by using extensions and code snippets. The snippets and patterns contributed by other members help developers to accomplish common tasks like database access, caching, file upload and authentication without writing any additional code.

8) Pyramid

Despite being a lightweight and simple Python web framework, Pyramid is hugely popular among programmers due to its high and rapid performance. The open source framework can be used for creating a variety of applications. Once the standard Python development environment is set up, the developers can use Pyramid to build the applications rapidly. Pyramid further allows users to take advantage of an independent Model-view-controller (MVC) structure. At the same time, they can further take advantage of other frameworks by integrating them with Pyramid.

9) Web.py

As a simple but powerful web framework for Python, web.py helps programmers to build a variety of modern web applications rapidly. The combination of simple architecture and impressive development potential further helps users to overcome some of the common restrictions and inconveniences in web development. It still lacks many features provided by other modern web frameworks. But developers can easily integrate web.py with other frameworks to avail a number of advanced features and functionality.

10) TurboGears

As a highly-scalable web application development framework for Python, TurboGears helps users to eliminate restrictions and limitations within the development environment. It can be used as a micro-framework or full-stack framework. It further provides a flexible object relationship mapper (ORM), along with supporting several databases, multiple data exchange formats, and horizontal data partitioning. The developers can further use the new widget system provided by TurboGears to effectuate development of AJAX-heavy web applications.

On the whole, the Python developers have option to choose from many frameworks. Some of these frameworks effectuate development of GUI desktop applications, whereas others help programmers to build modern websites and web application rapidly. At the same time, the developers also have option to use certain frameworks to write mobile apps in Python. That is why; it becomes essential for the developer to assess the suitability of each framework for his project based on its features and functionality. The user can also consider integrating the framework with other frameworks and tools to avail more advanced features and functionality.

CHAPTER 10

ROLE OF PYTHON IN IMAGE APPLICATIONS

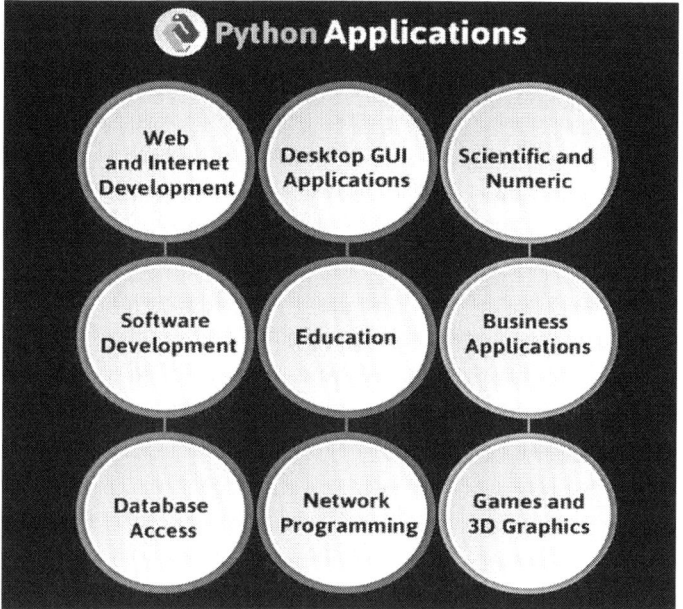

Python is a high level programming language that lets you work more quickly and integrate your systems more effectively. 90% of people prefer Python over other technology because of its simplicity, reliability and easy interfacing. It is often compared to Lisp, Tcl, Perl, Ruby, C#, Visual Basic, Visual Fox Pro, Scheme or Java. It can be easily interfaced with C/ObjC/Java/Fortran. It runs on all major operating systems such as Windows, Linux/Unix, OS/2, Mac, Amiga, etc. Day by day we can see a rapid growth in Python Development.

Python supports multiple programming paradigms and modules. Python is also supported for the Internet Communications Engine (ICE) and many other integration technologies. It is packed with rich libraries and many add-on packages to tackle specific tasks. Python is friendly language you can learn it easily. Python used in many business, government, non-profit organizations, Google search engine, YouTube, NASA, the New York Stock Exchange, etc. Python is often used as a scripting language, but is also used in a wide range of non-scripting contexts. It provides very clear and readable syntax. You can easily write programs using this language. The Python code runs more than fast enough for most applications.

It is used in a wide variety of application domains. Python is an excellent language for learning object orientation.

Applications written in Python are:

- Web Applications (Django, Pylons)
- Games (Eve Online - MMORPG).
- 3D CAD/CAM.
- Image Applications.
- Science and Education Applications.
- Software Development (Trac for Project Management).
- Object Databases (ZODB / Durus).
- Network Programming (Bittorent).
- Mobile applications.
- Audio/Video Applications.
- Office Applications.
- Console Applications.
- Enterprise Applications.
- File Formats.
- Internet Applications.
- Python in Image Applications

Always images play a big role in reaching the audience than the words in the web application field. Because a picture is worth a thousand words. Generally some users can satisfy with the existing images but some users want to make some creativity or changes to an image. In order to fulfil their demands Python provides various programs. Let's see how Python used in imaging applications

Gnofract 4D is a flexible fractal generation program, allows user to create beautiful images called fractals. Based on mathematical principles, the computer created the images automatically, include the Mandelbrot and Julia sets and many more. It doesn't mean that you need to do math for creating the images. Instead you can use your mouse to create more images as per your wish. Basically it runs on Unix-based systems such as Linux and FreeBSD and can also be run on Mac OS X. It is very easy to use, very fast, and flexible with an unlimited number of fractal functions and vast amount of options. It is a widely used open source program.

Gogh is a PyGTK-based painting program or image editor with support for pressure-sensitive tablets/devices.

ImgSeek is a photo collection manager and viewer with content-based search. It has many features. If you want to find a particular item, you simply sketch the image or you can use another image in your collection. It provides you with what you exactly need.

VPython is the Python programming language plus a 3D graphics module called "visual". By using it you can easily create objects in 3D space and animations etc. It helps you to display the objects in a window. VPython allows the programmers to focus more on the computational aspect of their programs.

MayaVi is a scientific visualization program based on the Visualization Toolkit (VTK), supports volume visualization of data via texture and ray cast mappers. It is easy to use. It can be imported as a Python module from other Python programs and can also be scripted from the Python interpreter.

The Python Applications used in different ways in the image application. Not only in this field, it also used in various types of applications.

CHAPTER 11

LOGISTIC REGRESSION WITH L2 REGULARIZATION IN PYTHON

L2 Regularization

$$E = \frac{1}{2} * \sum (t_k - o_k)^2 + \frac{1}{2} * \sum w_i^2$$

plain error — weight penalty

elegant math — simple math

$$\frac{\partial E}{\partial w_{jk}}$$

$$\Delta w_{jk} = \eta * \left[x_j * (o_k - t_k) * o_k * (1 - o_k) \right] + \left[\lambda * w_{jk} \right]$$

learning rate — signal

Logistic regression is used for binary classification problems -- where you have some examples that are "on" and other examples that are "off." You get as input a training set; which has some examples of each class along with a label saying whether each example is "on" or "off". The goal is to learn a model from the training data so that you can predict the label of new examples that you haven't seen before and don't know the label of.

For one example, suppose that you have data describing a bunch of buildings and earthquakes (E.g., year the building was constructed, type of material used, strength of earthquake,etc), and you know whether each building collapsed ("on") or not ("off") in each past earthquake. Using this data, you'd like to make predictions about whether a given building is going to collapse in a hypothetical future earthquake.

One of the first models that would be worth trying is logistic regression.
 Coding it up

I wasn't working on this exact problem, but I was working on something close. Being one to practice what I preach, I started looking for a dead simple Python logistic regression class. The only requirement is that I wanted it to support L2 regularization (more on this later). I'm also sharing this code with a bunch of other people on many platforms, so I wanted as few dependencies on external libraries as possible.

I couldn't find exactly what I wanted, so I decided to take a stroll down memory lane and implement it myself. I've written it in C++ and Matlab before but never in Python.

I won't do the derivation, but there are plenty of good explanations out there to follow if you're not afraid of a little calculus. Just do a little Googling for "logistic regression derivation." The big idea is to write down the probability of the data given some setting of internal parameters, then to take the derivative, which will tell you how to change the internal parameters to make the data more likely. Got it? Good.

For those of you out there that know logistic regression inside and out, take a look at how short the train() method is. I really like how easy it is to do in Python.

Regularization

I caught a little indirect flak during March madness season for talking about how I regularized the latent vectors in my matrix-factorization model of team offensive and defensive strengths when predicting outcomes in NCAA basketball. Apparently people thought I was talking nonsense -- crazy, right?

But seriously, guys -- regularization is a good idea.

Let me drive home the point. Take a look at the results of running the code (linked at the bottom).

Take a look at the top row.

On the left side, you have the training set. There are 25 examples laid out along the x axis, and the y axis tells you if the example is "on" (1) or "off" (0). For each of these examples, there's a vector describing its attributes that I'm not showing. After training the model, I ask the model to ignore the known training set labels and to estimate the probability that each label is "on" based only on the examples's description vectors and what the model has learned (hopefully things like stronger earthquakes and older buildings increase the likelihood of collapse). The probabilities are shown by the red X's. In the top left, the red X's are right on top of the blue dots, so it is very sure about the labels of the examples, and it's always correct.

Now on the right side, we have some new examples that the model hasn't seen before. This is called the test set. This is essentially the same as the left side, but the model knows nothing about the test set class labels (yellow dots). What you see is that it still does a decent job of predicting the labels, but there are some troubling cases where it is very confident and very wrong. This is known as overfitting.

This is where regularization comes in. As you go down the rows, there is stronger L2 regularization -- or equivalently, pressure on the internal parameters to be zero. This has the effect of reducing the model's certainty. Just because it can perfectly reconstruct the training set doesn't mean that it has everything figured out. You can imagine that if you were relying on this model to make important decisions, it would be desirable to have at least a bit of regularization in there.

And here's the code. It looks long, but most of it is to generate the data and plot the results. The bulk of the work is done in the train() method, which is only three (dense) lines. It requires numpy, scipy, and pylab.

* For full disclosure, I should admit that I generated my random data in a way such that it is susceptible to overfitting, possibly making logistic-regression-without-regularization look worse than it is.

The Python Code

```
from scipy.optimize.optimize import fmin_cg, fmin_bfgs, fmin

import numpy as np

def sigmoid(x):

    return 1.0 / (1.0 + np.exp(-x))

class SyntheticClassifierData():
```

```python
def __init__(self, N, d):
    """ Create N instances of d dimensional input vectors and a 1D
    class label (-1 or 1). """

    means = .05 * np.random.randn(2, d)

    self.X_train = np.zeros((N, d))

    self.Y_train = np.zeros(N)

    for i in range(N):
```

```python
        if np.random.random() > .5:

            y = 1

        else:

            y = 0

        self.X_train[i, :] = np.random.random(d) + means[y, :]

        self.Y_train[i] = 2.0 * y - 1




    self.X_test = np.zeros((N, d))

    self.Y_test = np.zeros(N)

    for i in range(N):
```

```python
        if np.random.randn() > .5:

            y = 1

        else:

            y = 0

        self.X_test[i, :] = np.random.random(d) + means[y, :]

        self.Y_test[i] = 2.0 * y - 1

class LogisticRegression():

    """ A simple logistic regression model with L2 regularization (zero-mean

    Gaussian priors on parameters). """
```

```python
def __init__(self, x_train=None, y_train=None, x_test=None, y_test=None,
             alpha=.1, synthetic=False):

    # Set L2 regularization strength
    self.alpha = alpha

    # Set the data.
    self.set_data(x_train, y_train, x_test, y_test)

    # Initialize parameters to zero, for lack of a better choice.
```

```python
self.betas = np.zeros(self.x_train.shape[1])

def negative_lik(self, betas):

    return -1 * self.lik(betas)

def lik(self, betas):

    """ Likelihood of the data under the current settings of parameters. """


    # Data likelihood

    l = 0

    for i in range(self.n):

        l += log(sigmoid(self.y_train[i] *
```

```
            np.dot(betas, self.x_train[i,:])))


    # Prior likelihood

    for k in range(1, self.x_train.shape[1]):

        l -= (self.alpha / 2.0) * self.betas[k]**2


    return l

def train(self):

    """ Define the gradient and hand it off to a scipy gradient-based

    optimizer. """
```

```python
# Define the derivative of the likelihood with respect to beta_k.
# Need to multiply by -1 because we will be minimizing.
dB_k = lambda B, k : np.sum([-self.alpha * B[k] +
                             self.y_train[i] * self.x_train[i, k] *
                             sigmoid(-self.y_train[i] *
                             np.dot(B, self.x_train[i,:]))
                             for i in range(self.n)]) * -1
```

```python
# The full gradient is just an array of componentwise derivatives
dB = lambda B : np.array([dB_k(B, k)
                          for k in range(self.x_train.shape[1])])

# Optimize
self.betas = fmin_bfgs(self.negative_lik, self.betas, fprime=dB)

def set_data(self, x_train, y_train, x_test, y_test):
```

```python
    """ Take data that's already been generated.
"""



    self.x_train = x_train

    self.y_train = y_train

    self.x_test = x_test

    self.y_test = y_test

    self.n = y_train.shape[0]

def training_reconstruction(self):

    p_y1 = np.zeros(self.n)

    for i in range(self.n):
```

```
        p_y1[i] = sigmoid(np.dot(self.betas, self.x_train[i,:]))


    return p_y1

    def test_predictions(self):

        p_y1 = np.zeros(self.n)

        for i in range(self.n):

            p_y1[i] = sigmoid(np.dot(self.betas, self.x_test[i,:]))


        return p_y1
```

```python
def plot_training_reconstruction(self):
    plot(np.arange(self.n), .5 + .5 * self.y_train, 'bo')
    plot(np.arange(self.n), self.training_reconstruction(), 'rx')
    ylim([-.1, 1.1])

def plot_test_predictions(self):
    plot(np.arange(self.n), .5 + .5 * self.y_test, 'yo')
    plot(np.arange(self.n), self.test_predictions(), 'rx')
```

```
        ylim([-.1, 1.1])

if __name__ == "__main__":

    from pylab import *

    # Create 20 dimensional data set with 25 points -- this will be
    # susceptible to overfitting.
    data = SyntheticClassifierData(25, 20)

    # Run for a variety of regularization strengths
    alphas = [0, .001, .01, .1]
    for j, a in enumerate(alphas):
```

```
# Create a new learner, but use the same data for each run

lr = LogisticRegression(x_train=data.X_train, y_train=data.Y_train,
                        x_test=data.X_test, y_test=data.Y_test,
                        alpha=a)

print "Initial likelihood:"
print lr.lik(lr.betas)

# Train the model
```

```
lr.train()



# Display execution info

print "Final betas:"

print lr.betas

print "Final lik:"

print lr.lik(lr.betas)



# Plot the results

subplot(len(alphas), 2, 2*j + 1)
```

```
lr.plot_training_reconstruction()

ylabel("Alpha=%s" % a)

if j == 0:

    title("Training set reconstructions")




subplot(len(alphas), 2, 2*j + 2)

lr.plot_test_predictions()

if j == 0:

    title("Test set predictions")

show() .
```

CHAPTER 12

CAN PYTHON WEB APPLICATIONS BE TESTED USING SELENIUM?

Python is currently more popular than other modern programming languages. The interpreted and object-oriented programming language is also hugely popular among developers across the world as a strong server side scripting language. As Python enables developers to express concepts by writing less and readable code, it becomes easier for programmers to reduce the development time significantly. At the same time, the developers also have option to use popular web frameworks like Django to create high-performing and complex Python web applications rapidly. However, the developers still need to assess the look, feel and performance of the Python web application thoroughly to boost its popularity and profitability.

While testing the internet applications the developers have option to choose from a number of browser automation tools like PAMIE, PyXPCOM, windmill, SST and Selenium. But most developers prefer Selenium to other frameworks to test their Python web applications efficiently. Unlike other web browser automation tools, Selenium allows testing professionals to write test scripts in a number of languages including Python, C#, Java, PHP, Ruby and Python. So the testers have option to test the Python web application by writing test scripts in Python. There are also a number of reasons why developers across the world use Selenium for testing Python web applications.

Why QA Professionals Prefer Using Selenium for Testing Python Web Applications?

Supports Major Operating Systems and Web Browsers

At present, Selenium supports all major operating systems and web browsers. The framework currently supports both Microsoft Windows and Linux. Likewise, it is compatible with most popular web browsers like Firefox, Chrome, Internet Explorer, Safari and Opera. The compatibility makes it easier for QA professionals to test the Python web application tools across multiple platforms and web browsers without writing separate codes, or using additional test automation tools. Selenium further comes with features to generate and execute test scripts automatically across different web browsers and systems simultaneously.

Allows Users to Create Complete Test Automation Suite

The Selenium testing professionals can create a complete test automation suite by combining

Selenium WebDriver and Selenium IDE. They can use Selenium WebDriver to quickly create browser-based regression automation suites and tests. Further, they can scale and distribute the test scripts across multiple environments. The Selenium IDE, on the other hand, makes it easier for testers to create bug-reproduction scripts rapidly. Thus, the QA professionals can combine distinct parts of Selenium to create a complete test automation tool, without requiring any licensed or third-party APIs.

EXECUTES TESTS FASTER

To identify all bugs and performance issues in the web applications, QA professionals have to perform tests repeatedly and frequently. But the testers also have to complete all tests within a limited amount of time. Selenium allows testing professionals to take advantage of cloud-based testing grids to boost the performance of their test runs. In addition to optimizing the test infrastructure, these tools further enable testers to run parallel tests. Thus, it becomes easier for the testers to execute tests quickly and repeatedly. The testers also have option to choose from several open source cloud-based functional testing grids to avoid increased project overheads.

Requires Basic HTML Concepts

Selenium supports a number of modern programming languages. But while testing a Python web application, it requires only basic HTML concepts. HTML is used for describing a web page, whereas individual HTML tags represent document content. Thus, HTML tags decide how the content is appears on the web browsers. Selenium divides the HTML elements or attributes into three distinct categories, i.e., single, group and customized. It locates single elements by their id, link or link text, whereas the group elements are identified based on combined values or index property. So it becomes easier for testers to find out the location of the defect or bug. The feature makes it easier for them to identify the exact bugs and performance issues quickly.

Helps Testers to Address Maintainability Issues

In addition to creating and executing test scripts quickly, QA professionals are also required to maintain the test cases effectively. Selenium helps testers to overcome maintainability issues by structuring the automated test code using a pattern called page objects. The page objects focuses on the structure of HTML code of a particular web page instead of checking how the services are implemented. Thus, testers can take advantage of page objects to locate the code easily, navigate between various web pages smoothly, and making changes only once. As most Selenium code will be located inside page objects, the testers can easily increase the code base without adding fresh Selenium code.

Provides Selenium Python API

As noted earlier, Python supports several programming languages including Python. So the testers have option to write test scripts in Python. Also, they can use Selenium Python API to write acceptance and functional tests by accessing Selenium WebDrivers like common, support, chrome, Firefox, ie, remote and phantomjs. The most recent version of the API further supports multiple versions of Python including 3.2, 3.3, 3.4 and 2.7. It can further be accessed simply by downloading and installing the Selenium Python bindings. Thus, an organization can leverage the skills of existing Python programmers to perform acceptance and functional testing efficiently.

Works with several testing frameworks
While testing the Python web application with Selenium, QA professionals have option to use a number of test framework. At present, the portable web browser automation framework works with Pytest, PyUnit, unittest, and robot framework. As a part of Python 2.1 standard library, PyUnit enables testers to write tests easily, and execute multiple tests in text or GUI mode. Likewise, pytest comes with a number of features that help testers to write better programs. So the QA professional can take advantage of these test frameworks to ensure that the Python web application delivers flawless user experience across many web browsers.

Python is an open source programming language, whereas Selenium is an open source web browser automation tool. Thus, organizations can use the programming language and web testing tool together to bring down the project costs.

However, the combination will further enable them test the application across major web browsers within a stipulated amount of time.

CHAPTER 13

PERL AND PYTHON

Both Python and Perl are mature, open source, general purpose, high level, and interpreted programming languages. But the usage statistics posted on various websites depict that Python is currently more popular than Perl. Hence, a software developer can enhance his career prospects by switching form Perl to Python.

A beginner can further learn and use Python programming language without putting extra time and effort. However, you must not switch to a new programming language just because its popularity and usage. You must keep in mind the major differences between the two programming languages while deciding about migrating from Perl to Python.

Points You Must Keep in Mind while Switching from Perl to Python

1) Design Goal

Perl was originally designed as a scripting language to simplify report processing capabilities. Hence, it comes with built-in text processing capability. On the other hand, Python was designed initially as a hobby programming language. But it was designed with features to help programmers build applications with concise, readable and reusable code. The two programming languages still differ in the category of features and performance.

2) Syntax Rules

The syntax rules of both Python and Perl are influenced by several other programming languages. For instance, Perl borrows features from a number of programming languages including C, shell script, sed, AWK and Lisp. Likewise, Python implements functional programming features in a manner similar to Lisp. But Python is hugely popular among modern programming languages due to its simple syntax rules. In addition to being easy to use, the syntax rules of Python further enable programmers to except many concepts with less and readable code.

3) Family of Languages

Perl belongs to a family of high-level programming languages that includes Perl 5 and Perl 6. The versions 5 and 6 of Perl are compatible with each other. A developer can easily migrate from Perl 5 to Perl 6 without putting extra time and effort. The programmers have option to choose from two distinct versions of Python - Python 2 and Python 2. But the two versions of Python are not compatible with each other. Hence, a programmer has to choose from two distinct versions of the programming language.

4) Ways to Achieve Same Results

Python enables programmers to express concepts without writing longer lines of code. But it requires programmers to accomplish tasks or achieve results in a specific and single way. ON the other hand, Perl enable programmers to accomplish a single task or achieve the same results in a number of ways. Hence, many programmers find Perl to be more flexible than Python. But the multiple ways to achieve the same result often make the code written in Perl messy and application difficult to maintain.

5) Web Scripting Language

Perl was originally designed as a UNIX scripting language. Many developers use Perl as a scripting language to avail its built-in text processing capabilities. However, there are many web developers who complain that Perl is slower than other widely used scripting language. Python is also used widely by programmers for web application development. But it lacks built-in web development capabilities. Hence, developers have to avail various frameworks and tools to write web applications in Python efficiently and rapidly.

6) Web Application Frameworks

Most developers nowadays avail the tools and features provided by various frameworks to build web applications efficiently and rapidly. Perl web programmers have option to choose from an array of frameworks including Catalyst, Dancer, Mojolicious, Poet, Interchange, Jifty, and Gantry. Likewise, the web developers also have option to use a number of Python web frameworks including Django, Flask, Pyramid, Bottle and Cherrypy. However, the number of Python web framework is much higher than the number of Perl web frameworks.

7) Usage

As mentioned earlier, both Python and Perl are general-purpose programming languages. Hence, each programming language is used for developing a variety of software applications. Perl is used widely for graphic and network programming, system administration, and development of finance and biometric applications. But Python comes with a robust standard library simplifies web application development, scientific computing, big data solution development, and artificial intelligence tasks. Hence, developers prefer using Python for development of advanced and mission-critical software applications.

8) Performance and Speed

A number of studies have shown than Python is slower than other programming languages like Java and C++. Hence, developers frequently explore ways to enhance the execution speed of Python code. Some developers even replace default Python runtime with their own custom runtime to make the Python applications run faster. Many programmers even find Perl to be faster than Python. Many web developers use Perl as a scripting language make the web applications faster, and deliver enhanced user experience.

9) Structured Data Analysis

At present, big data is one of the hottest trends in software development. Many enterprises nowadays build custom applications for collecting, storing, and analyzing huge amount of structured and unstructured data. The PDL provided by Perl enables developers to analyze big data. The built-in text processing capability of Perl further simplifies and speeds up analysis of huge amount of structured data. But Python is used widely by programmers for data analysis. The developers further take advantage of robust Python libraries like Numpy to process and analyze huge volumes of data in a faster and more efficient way.

10) JVM Interoperability

At present, Java is one of the programming languages that are used widely for development of desktop, web, and mobile applications. In comparison to Perl, Python interoperates with Java Virtual Machine (JVM) seamlessly and efficiently. Hence, the developers have option to write Python code than runs smoothly on JVM, while taking advantage of robust Java APIs and objects. The interoperability helps programmers to build application by targeting the popular Java platform, while writing code in Python instead of Java.

11) Advanced Object Oriented Programming

Both Perl and Python are object-oriented programming languages. But Python implements advanced object oriented programming languages in a better way than Perl. While writing code in Perl, programmers still need to use packages instead of classes. Python programmers can write high quality and modular code by using classes and objects. Many developers find it difficult to keep the code simple and readable while writing object oriented code in Perl. But Perl makes it easier for programmers to accomplish a variety of tasks simply by using one liners on the command line.

12) Text Processing Capability

Unlike Python, Perl was designed with built-in text processing capabilities. Hence, many programmers prefer using Perl for report generation. Perl further makes it easier for programmers to perform regex and string comparison operations like matching, replacement, and substitution. It further does not require developers to write additional code to perform exception handling and I/O operations. Hence, many programmers prefer Perl to Python while building applications that need to process textual data or generate reports.

On the whole, a large number of modern software developers prefer Python to Perl. But there are a number of programming languages - Java, C, C++ and C# - which are currently more popular than both Perl and Python. Also, Python, like other technologies, also has its own shortcomings. For instance, you will be required to use Python frameworks while writing applications in the programming language. Hence, you must keep in mind the pros and cons of both programming languages before migrating from Perl to Python.

CHAPTER 14

APPS BUILT WITH PYTHON

Over its almost 30 years of existence, Python has become one of the most popular programming languages. But if most startups once used it because of its simplicity and low cost, modern giants like Instagram or Spotify use Python and the Django framework to create smooth working experiences. Famously, Django provides fast work processes, clean design, and transparent functionality, among many other advantages. It allows developers at all levels to focus on writing their apps instead of reinventing the wheel (or fixing it, for that matter). On top of that, it's free, open source, and has gathered a mighty community of developers over the years. Large companies appreciate this. To give you an example, let's take a look at some apps written in Python that you probably didn't know about.

Instagram

As you know, this is the app that changed the world of digital photography, made it instant, more accessible and widespread, expanded lines of creativity and defined new rules in marketing. It allows users to take pictures, edit and share them online using a camera as simple as a smartphone. With 400 million active users per day, it obviously negates any notion that apps built in Python are not really scalable. According to Instagram engineer Hui Ding, Instagram's engineering motto is "Do the simple things first"—and this is what Python allows developers to do. For them, it's user-friendly, simple, clean, and favors pure pragmatism. And since it's so popular, growing an engineering team is a lot easier

Pinterest

Ranking third behind Facebook and Twitter, Pinterest is a social network that allows users to bookmark images, collect and share them with other users. As one of the web's most-used apps, Pinterest relies on Python and Django to rapidly deal with large amounts of content. In fact, this website has used Python since day one.

Disqus

This commenting plug-in is a simple and effective way to engage an audience and fuel discussion while controlling incoming content by efficiently moderating the comments. Allowing multiple sign-in options and cross-site notifications, this app serves audiences with all kinds of preferences. In this case, Python makes full use of Django's security features and regular security patches.

Spotify

Spotify is the world's largest streaming service, with annual revenue of over €4 billion. This makes it a major market player and also one of the top Python users among businesses. The company chose to work with Python because of the development speed and advanced data analytics that the language offers. This enables Spotify to manage functions such as Radio and Discover, which are based on the personal musical preferences of users.

Dropbox

Another top app built in Python is Dropbox. The popular file-hosting service recently moved from Python 2.7 to Python 3 in one of the largest Python 3 migrations ever. One of the most popular desktop apps in the world, Dropbox can be installed on Windows, macOS, and some flavors of Linux. It's a good thing that Python is portable and works on many platforms, from PC and Linux to PlayStation.

Uber

A ride-hailing service that also offers food delivery, peer-to-peer ridesharing and bicycle-sharing (among other services), Uber has a lot of calculations to do. Think about it: the company operates in 785 metropolitan areas worldwide and is estimated to have 100 million users. That's a lot of math. But again, Python handles large amounts of data and is easy to learn and work with, which are two reasons why Python is so popular. These benefits make it an obvious choice for companies whose applications need to be reliable, secure and rely on developers around the world to maintain it.

Reddit

The American social news aggregator and discussion website Reddit also runs on Python, even though originally it was written in Common Lisp. After looking for wider access to code libraries and greater development flexibility, Reddit made the switch. If you look at it, this website is somewhat of an anthill. With about 542 million monthly visitors as of February 2018, Reddit is one of the most impressive Python app examples. Registered users post content such as text, video, or images in thousands of categories, and vote it up and down. Using a localization management platform, users help translate Reddit into 89 different languages. Again, Python manages the workload and complex functionality thanks to its "batteries included" approach.

What can we say? That's a powerful portfolio! As we mentioned earlier, Python used to be a language for rough drafts and startup development because it was simple and cheap. But usually, the simplest solutions are the most reliable ones. The more parts a mechanism has, the higher the chances of something breaking or someone messing up—which many large companies learned the hard way. That's why they chose to work with Python, and why so many of the world's most popular apps are built in Python. Python has proven that you can build an amazing product with simple, time-honored tools—as long as you create it for the users and don't have to dig into overcomplicated code. (Unless, of course, you want to.)

CHAPTER 15

TOOLS TO RUN PYTHON ON ANDROID

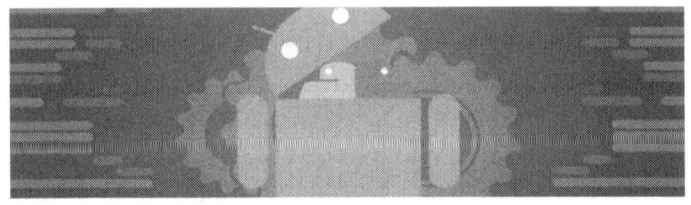

Python has proven itself as a highly capable language—approachable for newcomers, but powerful in the hands of experts. Why shouldn't you be able to use Python everywhere that you need to tell a computer to do something? And shouldn't your tools exploit all the capabilities of Python as a language, not just the bits that map nicely to a C binding?

Modern computing doesn't happen in an 80x25 console window. It happens on phones, tablets, and desktop machines with rich user interfaces. Shouldn't you be able to use Python in all those locations, and exploit the unique capabilities of those platforms?

End users shouldn't have to care what language their tools are written in. And that starts with looking and behaving like completely native tools. Native appearance, native behavior, delivered in the way a native app is delivered. Why shouldn't your Python tools fit in just as well as a native tool?

There are several ways to use Python on Android.

BeeWare
BeeWare is a collection of tools for building native user interfaces

This is what BeeWare provides. Tools to help you write Python code with a rich, native user interface; and the libraries and support code necessary to get that code running on iOS, Android, macOS, Linux, Windows, tvOS, and more.

Open source

The Open Source development process has proven itself to be the most reliable way to develop robust and reliable software. That's why the entire BeeWare suite of tools are BSD licensed, and available for all to use and modify.

Chaquopy

Chaquopy is a plugin for Android Studio's Gradle-based build system.

Chaquopy enables you to freely intermix Java and Python in your app, using whichever language is best for your needs:

With the Python API , you can write an app partly or entirely in Python. The complete Android API and user interface toolkit are directly at your disposal.

Chaquopy works within Android's standard build system:

If you use Android Studio, you can start using Chaquopy in 5 minutes with no change to your existing development process.

Download and installation are automated via Gradle.

To get started:

Try out the demo app for Python 2 or Python 3.

Browse example source code on GitHub.

Or view the documentation.

Kivy

Kivy is a cross-platform OpenGL-based user interface toolkit.

You can run Kivy applications on Android, on (more or less) any device with OpenGL ES 2.0 (Android 2.2 minimum). This is standard on modern devices; Google reports the requirement is met by 99.9% of devices.

Kivy APKs are normal Android apps that you can distribute like any other, including on stores like the Play store. They behave properly when paused or restarted, may utilise Android services and have access to most of the normal java API as described below.

Follow the instructions below to learn how to package your app for Android, debug your code on the device, and use Android APIs such as for vibration and reading sensors.

The Kivy project provides all the necessary tools to package your app on Android, including building your own standalone APK that may be distributed on a market like the Play store. This is covered fully in the Create a package for Android documentation.

Using Android APIs

Although Kivy is a Python framework, the Kivy project maintains tools to easily use the normal java APIs, for everything from vibration to sensors to sending messages through SMS or email.

For new users, we recommend using Plyer. For more advanced access or for APIs not currently wrapped, you can use Pyjnius directly. Kivy also supplies an android module for basic Android functionality.

User contributed Android code and examples are available on the Kivy wiki.

Pyqtdeploy

Pyqtdeploy is a tool for deploying PyQt applications. It supports deployment to desktop platforms (Linux, Windows and OS X) and to mobile platforms (iOS and Android).

pyqtdeploy works by taking the individual modules of a PyQt application, freezing them, and then placing them in a Qt resource file that is converted to C++ code by Qt's rcc tool. Python's standard library is handled in the same way.

pyqtdeploy also generates a Qt .pro file that describes all the generated C++ code. From this Qt's qmake tool is used to generate a platform-specific Makefile which will then generate a single executable. Further Qt and/or platform specific tools can then be used to convert the executable to a platform specific deployable package.

pyqtdeploy requires PyQt5 and Python v3.2 or later to be installed.

PyQt4 and PyQt5 applications written using Python v2.6 and later and Python v3.3 and later are supported.

pyqtdeploy is released under the BSD license.

QPython

QPython is an on-device script engine and development environment.

In most cases, script can get your jobs done as good as the native application. Now you can make it with QPython's help.

QPython is a script engine which runs Python programs on android devices. It also can help developers develop android applications.

QPython includes a complete development kit which help you to develop programs with mobile provides regular Python console

SL4A

SL4A (Scripting Layer for Android), originally named ASE (Android Scripting Environment), is a set of "facades" which expose a greatly-simplified subset of the Android API.

SL4A brings scripting languages to Android by allowing you to edit and execute scripts and interactive interpreters directly on the Android device. These scripts have access to many of the APIs available to full-fledged Android applications, but with a greatly simplified interface that makes it easy to get things done.

Scripts can be run interactively in a terminal and in the background. Python, Perl, JRuby, Lua, BeanShell, JavaScript, Tcl, and shell are currently supported, and we're planning to add more. See the SL4A Video Help playlist on YouTube for various demonstrations of SL4A's features.

SL4A is designed for developers and is alpha quality software.

PySide

PySide (the Python binding for the Qt toolkit) has some preliminary support for Android.

The PySide project provides LGPL-licensed Python bindings for the Qt 4. It also includes complete toolchain for rapidly generating bindings for any Qt-based C++ class hierarchies. PySide Qt bindings allow both free open source and proprietary software development and ultimately aim to support Qt platforms.

Termux

Termux is an Android terminal emulator and Linux environment app that works directly with no rooting or setup required. A minimal base system is installed automatically—additional packages are available using the APT package manager.

CHAPTER 16

PYTHON AS A MOBILE APP DEVELOPMENT LANGUAGE

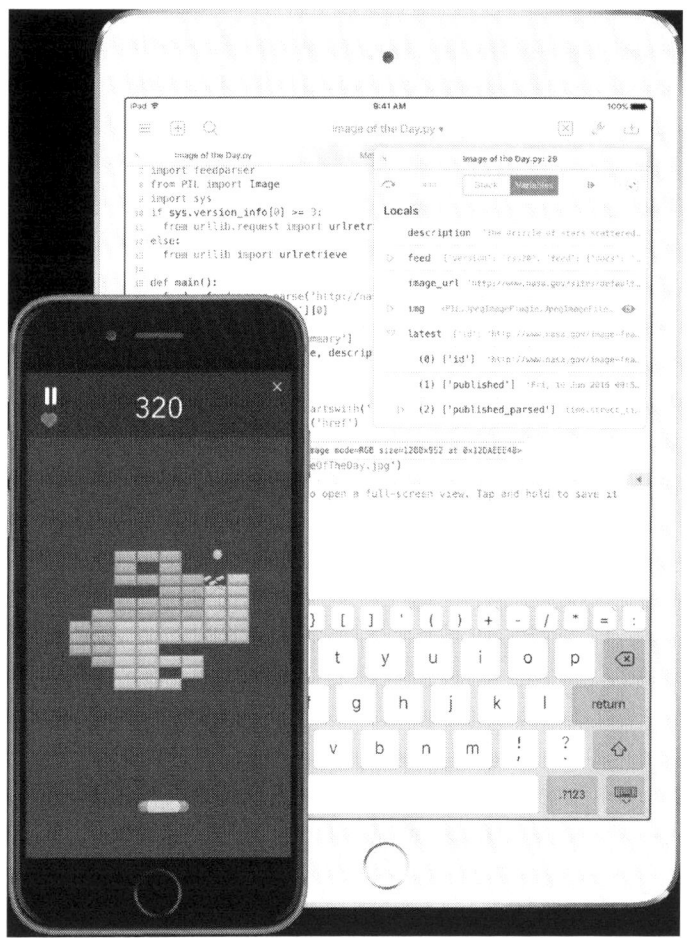

Why should you consider Python for mobile app development? These features make it easy to use to create expressive, quality apps.

Mobile has become one of the primary needs of today's generation. Therefore, it is quite impossible for people to live without mobile phones, as they play an important role in our lives. Recognizing this dependence, various mobile application development companies launch new applications frequently, in order to feed off this dependence.

This is a great business opportunity and is interesting, to say the least. The challenge, however, is not to jump on the mobile app development platform, but to choose the right programming language.

Why Python?

As we have several choices while selecting the best programming language, one of the easiest ways is to go for the most popular language. According to Codevaal, Python was the most popular coding language in 2014.

In comparison to other programming languages, Python is easier to learn, highly readable, and simple to implement as it has a clean syntax which requires less coding. It focuses on the business logic rather than basic facts of the language. Python is used in a wide variety of application domains as it can easily be connected with C, Objective-C, Java, or FORTRAN. It runs on all major operating systems, like Windows, Linux/Unix, OS/2, Mac, Amiga, etc. With the help of Python, we can create any type of mobile applications, like Calibre, OpenStack, Ubuntu Software Center, World of Tanks, Quora, BitTorrent, Reddit, Spotify, YouTube, Instagram, and many more.

Features of Python

There have been numerous programming languages introduced, all with their own specialties. For example, the top five popular languages: JavaScript, Python, C#, Android with Kotlin, and Go.

Before beginning with the deeper concept of Python for mobile development, let us take a look at its major features that give you reasons why should you choose Python for developing your apps in comparison to other tools:

Easy to read: For beginners, using a static language for the first time can be very difficult as it presents additional complexity. Python is dynamic language it instructs indentation, which aids readability.

Easy to code: Compared to other popular languages like Java and C++, Python is a much easier language to code. Anyone can learn Python within a few hours. It is called a programmer-friendly language as it is very easy to use.

Interpreted language: With some languages, like C++ or Java, we are always supposed to first compile it and then run it. But it's not the same with Python, as there is no need to compile it. This is because, internally, it converts one language to binary immediately.

Expressive: Python is an expressive language, considered a most outstanding feature as it helps to focus on the solution rather than the syntax.

Object-oriented language: Python's main focus is on objects, functions, and combining data. Python supports multiple inheritances. It also supports both object-oriented and procedure-orientated programming.

Python-iOS-support (CPython compiled for use on iOS)

VOC (A CPython bytecode to Java class file transpiler)

Python-iOS-template (a cookie-cutter template for iOS projects)

Python-Android-template (a cookie-cutter template for Android projects)

Briefcase (a distutils extension for packaging Python projects as apps)

Rubicon-ObjC (a bridge between Objective-C and Python)

Toga (a cross-platform native widget library)

The above tools were in the early phase of development, however, they are mature enough to demonstrate that the objectives of developing mobile apps in Python are neither an illusion nor a mirage.

Why Python for Mobile Development?

Python has the potential to run on any of the major operating systems such as OS/2, Linux/Unix, Mac, Amiga, Windows, etc.

The language offers a concept with the intention to allow obstacle-free programs on a small or large scale.

There is a variety of tools provided by Python for both developers and system administrators.

Due to Python's ability to be flexible and dynamic, users like Google, Yahoo, and IBM find it fun to work with.

The development and portability rate in Python are very high, which allows the same application to operate across platforms.

Python consists of rich libraries and many other packages to tackle a particular task.

Role of Python in Mobile Development
Mobile application development has become a major business sector because of its expanding scope. The cross-platform Python framework works for Android, Windows 7, Linux, and Mac. It is a perfect tool for writing simple scripts and complex multi-threaded applications.

The interesting thing about Android having Python in it is the chance to use limitless lines of code already written and available for free. Developers for iPhone and Android apps use a number of cross-platform development techniques to provide their customer a great mobile application.

MobiCart, RhoMobile, SwebApps, PhoneGap, Mippin, Appcelerator, AppMkr, Sencha Touch, GENWI, MoSync, WidgetPed, and Whoop are some of the top tools used for cross-formatting in mobile application development.

Python-Based Mobile Applications

Aarlogic C05/3: Ready-to-use GSM/GPS tracking PCB with a Python development board along with the support of test server based on Google Maps.

Pyroute: A GPS-capable mapping/routing application for mobile.

FoodPlus: A mobile food app which simplifies the process of food ordering and tracking, specially designed for food lovers.

AppBackup: An app for jailbroken iOS devices that lets one back up and restore the settings and data of App Store apps.

CHAPTER 17

PROGRAMMING LANGUAGES FOR MOBILE APP DEVELOPMENT

"Smartphone users touch their phones 2,617 times each day, and spend an average of 145 daily minutes on their mobile phones."

This is good news. Because you can now reach your target audience on the go.

Make no mistakes about it. Mobile users are one of the most active consumers.

If you can reach them via mobile apps, you can get them to try your product, purchase your product, or join your cause.

That's why you should continually try to generate new app ideas.

As mobile marketing continues to dominate the digital marketing realm, a lot of businesses are capitalizing on the latest mobile technology – mobile apps, to create brand awareness, acquire customers, and increase revenue.

Don't be left behind. Do you have the courage to take the plunge and build your own mobile app?

Truth is, if you're just starting out in this whole thing, you need the right tool to produce functional apps, and the right idea to get you the app valuation you want.

But more than that, you need the right programming language that's compatible with modern mobile platforms. Millions of people use smartphones today. So you need to build compatible mobile apps.

A report by Statista shows the staggering increase in the sales of smartphones from 2009 to 2015. The annual smartphone sales crossed 1.3 billion in 2015 with android being the most used OS for smartphones.

In another report, it's been predicted that the smartphone shipment worldwide will cross 1.6 billion by 2020. Again, Android is expected to rule the global smartphone market.

What do these numbers mean?

If you have to develop a mobile app, this is the most appropriate time. Whether you need to become a developer, or hire a professional mobile developer, this is the best time to get started.

Deciding to jump on the mobile app development bandwagon is not the challenge. The challenge is – choosing the right programming language.

Ultimately, you want to answer these questions:

Where do I begin?
Which programming language do I choose and why?
How do I master it?
What should I look for in a mobile developer?

These are just a few basic questions that come to mind as soon as you think of developing a mobile app.

There are several programming languages to choose from. One of the easiest ways is to select the most popular language. According to codeeval, Python is the most popular coding language.

The guide below will help you choose the right mobile app development coding language. By the end of this guide, you will have one thing absolutely clear in your mind – what language you will use.

BuildFire.js

BuildFire.js leverages the BuildFire SDK and Javascript to allow developers to rapidly build mobile apps with the power of the BuildFire backend.

With BuildFire already having plugins that cover 70% or more of the common business use cases, developers only need to build specific functionality that's unique to the client, rather than build the whole thing from scratch.

That means quicker builds, less headaches and more apps getting built.

BuildFire.js was built to have a flexible architecture to give developers the option to utilize any client-side Javascript framework they like including: jQuery, Angular, React, Underscore and many more.

Key features:

Easy to learn and works with existing frameworks you already use

Highly scalable

Short-cuts the development timeline by 40% or more

Resources:

Learn how to build your first app through the developer portal

Python

Let's talk about the most popular app development language – Python.

Python is a high-level programming language that is widely used in web development, app development, analyzing and computing scientific and numeric data, creating desktop GUIs, and for software development.

Python is the most taught programming language at the school and college level for the fact that it has several applications in real life.

The core philosophy of python language is:

Beautiful is better than ugly
Explicit is better than implicit
Simple is better than complex
Complex is better than complicated
Readability counts

If there is one language that you should learn for app development, it should be Python because it's easy-to-learn and it's great at readability.

Python is a powerful high-level language that can be used to create android and desktop apps from scratch. Just to give you a hint of how powerful this language is, Dropbox is created in Python.

If this isn't encouraging enough, here is a list of some other apps and websites developed in Python.

Calibre

OpenStack

Ubuntu Software Center

World of Tanks (I'm sure you have played it)

BitTorrent

Quora

Reddit

Spotify

Instagram

YouTube

The list can go on and on…

Well, the potential is there. You can create any type of mobile app with Python. Learning it is not a big deal since it is one of the easiest languages around.

You can get started right away.

Key features:

Processed at runtime by the interpreter

Object-oriented language

Easy-to-learn and master

Interactive language

Easy-to-read

Scalable

Supports GUI applications

Runs on Windows, Mac, Unix, and Linux

Resources:

Learn python the hard way is a free book to get started.

Write your first python application by Keenan Payne.

Codeacademy has a free course on Python.

Free Python tips.

Java

Java is the most used app development language. According to VersionEye, which tracks the open source software libraries, developers complete most projects in Java followed by Ruby.

According to PYPL Popularity, Java is the most searched language on Google worldwide in the current year.

Java stands at the number one place with 23.4% share, with Python at the second place with 13.7% share. The difference between the first and second place shows how popular Java is among developers.

Android OS is written in Java so if you learn Java, you will be able to create Android apps of all types and this will put you in the driving seat because you will be in control over the future of app technology.

Java is the most suitable mobile app development language because it runs on all the platforms including the all-famous Android.

Uses

Java is used in development of:

Android apps

Server apps

Web apps

Embedded space

Big data technology

Scientific apps

Websites

Games

Some of the most famous Java applications include:

ThinkFree cloud office
NASA world wind
Blu-ray Disc Association
UltraMixer
But nothing beats the Android operating system.

Java is believed to be everywhere since it is hooked to the Android operating system. It's open source, it's independent of platform, and has several uses in the real world.

Key features:

Object oriented language.
It runs on all the platforms.
Supports APIs that make integration a piece of cake.
It is easy-to-learn and read.
Hundreds of open source libraries available.
Easy to get expert help from Android communities.

Powerful IDEs make coding easy and error-free.

Resources

Android developer site

Java tutorials

Java tutorial for complete beginners is a free course on Udemy

More Java tutorials by Oracle

PHP

Hypertext Preprocessor (PHP) is a server-side scripting open source language. It was designed by Zend Technologies in 1995. It was developed for websites, but it's used for general purpose development today.

Besides server side scripting, it is used for command line scripting and for coding applications.

PHP primarily is a coding language used for creating dynamic websites, but you can create android and iOS apps in PHP, according to Zend.

With PHAP, it is possible to write complete android, iOS, and windows apps. Suman Tripathi shares a three-layered model for developing stunning apps in PHP for mobiles.

PHP is the most popular programming language as reported by Jobs Tractor. Java is the second most popular programming language.

magine if you learn PHP, you will be in a position to create dynamic websites, web applications, and all types of mobile apps. It's the single most used programming language out there that's supported and used by 78.6% developers.

Better yet, you can create stunning Facebook apps like Family Tree and eBuddy. You can create the next big app all in PHP, who knows?

In case you aren't aware, some of the biggest websites that you visit daily are coded in PHP such as Facebook, Wikipedia, Flickr, Yahoo, Tumblr, and several others.

[thrive_lead_lock id='14525']Hidden Content[/thrive_lead_lock]

Uses

Not just apps, you can use PHP for a whole lot of development including:

Ecommerce websites

Create GUI

Code project management tools

Create Facebook apps

Image processing

Mobile app development

Content management systems such as WordPress and Drupal

Dynamic websites

WordPress plugin development

Creating PDFs

Key features:

Open-source

Independent of platform

Uses procedural and object oriented

Easy-to-learn

Numerous applications and uses

Server compatibility

Easy database integration

Resources

Pear is the best repository for PHP extensions.

Official PHP manual.

PHP for beginners.

Video PHP tutorials.

Swift

If there is one programming language that has the potential to reshape the future, it is Swift.

It was released by Apple Inc. in June 2014 for iOS (and supporting systems) and Linux. It is the primary programming language used for developing iOS and OS X apps.

Swift is the fastest growing language, according to TNW. The demand for Swift developers has increased 600 percent making them the most hired developers.

Did I tell you that the Swift developers make serious money? Swift developers have the highest average salaries in the US.

There couldn't be any better time to learn and code a mobile app in Swift.

Google is also considering to make Swift its first-class language instead of Java. If Google shifts to Swift, the demand for Swift apps and developers will skyrocket and there will be no other competing language.

Swift means business.

One of the most famous examples of Swift apps is none other than SlideShare iOS app, which is completely built in Swift.

For now, Swift is only available for iOS development but since it works on Linux and is open source, which means it can be used by anyone. It is still new and those who will shift to Swift early will have the advantage.

Key features:

Extremely easy to learn especially if you know Objective-C.
It is open source.
It is a simplified version of Objective-C.
Easy-to-code.
Maintenance is super-easy.
It is the future of iOS development.
It needs less coding as compared to other languages.
Resources

Official Apple developer site
Beginner's guide for Swift
Introduction to Swift
Learnswift website

C#

C# is known as C Sharp. It is a multi-paradigm programming language, which is object and component oriented. It's a general-purpose programming language developed by Microsoft.

You can create pretty much anything in C# ranging from server applications to web services to games to mobile apps and more. If you're planning to develop a game app, C# is one of the best languages to go for since it is supported by Unity3D.

Most of the experts believe that the demand for C# is dipping and there are not enough jobs available in the market for C# developers.

Xamarin is the platform that has changed the expectations of the experts and the developers. It's an app building tool that makes it simpler for

C# developers to create apps for Android and iOS.

But mobile app development isn't the only thing that developers are doing, C# is used widely in business and productivity tools, enterprises, utilities, games, etc.

There's a lot of potential for C# since it's used for everything that you can think of: Visual Studio, AutoCAD, Office 365, and SharePoint are just a few examples of software built with C#. It's mostly used in the development of enterprise-level programs.

Just to give you a hint of how easy it is to create a mobile app in C# using Xamarin, Nish created an app in just one day.

You can create your next mobile app in C# fairly quickly.

Key features:

Easy-to-use and a simple language
Used extensively in the development of web applications and large tools
It is a type-safe language
It is scalable
Access to .NET framework
Resources

Microsoft's free tutorials
LearnCS is a nice resource
.NET blog

Objective-C

Objective-C is an object-oriented general-purpose programming language that is derived from C. Objective-C was the core programming language used by Apple for iOS and OS X development prior to Swift.

Though Swift is replacing Objective-C, but the queries at StackOverflow show that the developers are still working on Objective-C.

Same is the case with Github, developers are still creating their projects in Objective-C.

The transition will not be instant.

Objective-C isn't going anywhere any soon, says Paul Krill, for two main reasons. First, there has been a lot of investment in it in terms of apps. Second, the frameworks of the apps still rely on Objective-C even after the launch of Swift.

Therefore, learning and creating a mobile app in Objective-C will still pay off. You can create all types of apps in it, not really a big deal.

Key features:

Simple to use
You can use C++ and C while using Objective-C
It uses dynamic run-time
It supports dynamic typing
Works smoothly with Apple Inc.
Resources

Objective-C tutorial by Code School
Crash course by Ray W.
Training by Apple Inc.

C++

C++, pronounced as C Plus Plus, is a general purpose object-oriented programming language with low-level memory manipulation feature.

C++ inherits its syntax from C and it is an extension of the C. If you know how to use C, C++ will not be a big deal. The two languages share all the features but C++ is more comprehensive.

The demand for C++ has always been there. It's not just about developing mobile apps rather it is a powerful language that is used in all the sectors ranging from finance to manufacturing to banking and several others.

In terms of mobile apps, C++ has been doing exceptionally well since it helps develop cross-platform mobile apps easily with its unified debugging experience and powerful environment.

It can be used to create stunning apps for Android, Windows, and iOS.

Not just mobile apps, but C++ has the potential to create some of the biggest tools like Google Chrome, Amazon, PayPal, World of Warcraft, Photoshop, and many others.

Learning C++ means you will be able to smoothly code games, apps, and commercial software.

Some of the major uses of C++ (and C) include:

Development of operating systems

New programming language development

Graphics and designs

Game development

App development

Web browsers

Development of compilers for programming languages

Medical, mathematical, and engineering applications

Enterprise tools

Computation platforms

Key features

C++ is one of the most powerful languages out there with tons of features.

It is simple and efficient

Object oriented

Massive library

Portable

Extremely fast

Resources

The official website

LearnCPP is a great resource for beginners

CPlusPlus is a free resource

JavaScript

JavaScript is a high-level interpreted programming language. It is a multi-paradigm language that supports object-oriented and functional programming.

JavaScript is ranked third by the number of programming jobs it offers.

JavaScript is not primarily a language for app development instead, it is the language that is run by browsers which is used to develop and control web pages. Creating mobile apps with JavaScript is possible but it has to be used with CSS, HTML, and AJAX.

There are several frameworks that can be used to create a professional JavaScript app such as PhoneGap, jQuery Mobile, and Ionic.

Creating apps in JavaScript is easy because you have to code the app once and it can be released on all the platforms (Android, iOS, and Windows).

Key features:

One of the easiest languages out there that you can be learned in a few days.
Fast and efficient.
It is executed on the client-side which means it saves bandwidth by not using the server.
Used for dynamics and creating animations on otherwise dull and boring websites.
Resources

The official JavaScript website
JavaScript Track on Codecademy
Basics of JavaScript on Udacity

HTML5

HTML5 is the fifth version of HTML (HyperText Markup Language). HTML5 is used to present content on the internet.

HTML5 is not essentially a mobile app development language. In order to create an app in HTML5, it has to be used with other languages such as JavaScript.

You can create Android as well as iOS apps in HTML5. The only requirement is using a powerful framework such as PhoneGap.

Joe Wolf shares some great tips and reasons for creating HTML5 apps. You can create a mobile app in HTML5 (CSS and JavaScript) or you can use it in combination with APIs. In any case, HTML5 apps are responsive and work smoothly on all devices.

Code once, and use on multiple devices.

There are hundreds of web apps that are created in HTML5 that you use every single day. The all-famous Google Docs and Google Drive are mostly coded in HTML5. That's not all, the Zoho app collection has over 33 productivity apps and most of them are developed in HTML5.

So why bother creating a mobile app in HTML5 when there are more sophisticated programming languages available to choose from?

Here are a few reasons to learn and code in HTML5:

HTML5 has been fully adopted by mobile (and desktop) browsers.
Cross-browser support.

With its cross-browser support and responsiveness, anything created in HTML5 works on all devices painlessly.

Use canvas tag to develop games in HTML5.

Easy and clean coding.

It fully supports videos and audios.

Time to take HTML5 seriously.

Key features:

Easy-to-learn

Support for mobile

Responsive design with support for all the devices

Drag-and-drop feature

Resources

Learn HTML5 programming from scratch at Udemy.

HTML5 cheat sheet is a great resource for beginners.

HTML5 guide by Mozilla.

Ruby

Ruby is a general-purpose object-oriented programming language. It was developed by Yukihiro Matz Matsumoto in 1990s. It supports multiple paradigms.

The demand for Ruby developers is five times more than the demand for Python developers. It is the fastest growing programming language and an average Ruby developer earns $77K per project while some earn as high as $112K.

Analysis of over 50 repository servers shows that Ruby is the second language that has most projects completed while Java is at the top.

You cannot create a mobile app on Ruby without using a framework such as RubyMotion or Rhodes. Using one of these frameworks, you can create apps for Android, iOS, Windows, and OS X.

If there is one language that is easiest of them all, it is Ruby. You can create an app in 10 minutes on Ruby. It is not just easy to code but it is no less than a ghost.

Some of the biggest websites are coded in Ruby like Fiverr, Airbnb, Pixlr, Groupon, Basecamp, Scribd, Bloomberg, ThemeForest, and many others.

It is easy and insanely powerful. Why not use it to create a next level mobile app.

Key features:

It supports dynamic typing.

Object oriented language.

Easy coding. Anyone can do it.

Best for beginners.

Use existing codes.

Helpful community.

Resources

Ruby course by Code Academy.

Rail Casts.

Learn Ruby the hard way.

Perl

Perl is a combination of two languages (Perl 5 and Perl 6). This is a high-level dynamic programming language family. It uses features from other programming languages like C, sed, AWK, and others. Both Perl 5 and Perl 6 run and evolve independently.

Perl is used for a whole lot of applications such as automation, bioinformatics, website development, app development, games development, and others.

LiveJournal, IMDB, and Booking are a few most popular websites developed in Perl.

Developing Android apps in Perl is easier than before since Google now has its APK available for Perl developers.

For iOS app development, you have to use a framework. Catalyst, Dancer, and Mojo are the three most famous frameworks for Perl mobile app development.

Key features:

The most powerful feature of Perl is CPAN which is the comprehensive Perl archive network.
It is fast, reliable, and personal.
It is fun. Perl has the happiest users.
If you learn Perl, you will be operating in a low or no-competition zone.
Resources

How to build Perl on Android.
Official Perl website.
Perl for beginners.

Rust

Rust is a compiled programming language by Mozilla. It is a multiple paradigm general-purpose language.

Rust is like C and C++ but it is safer and better. It has a powerful management tool that makes it better than other programming languages such as Ruby and Python.

More than 64% of developers are using Rust which makes it quite a popular programming language among developers.

Rust is still a new language that is not fully mature but it has a great future. There are developers who are using Rust to create mobile apps such as John Gallagher who has created an iOS app in Rust.

Mozialla's browser engine, known as Servo, is developed in Rust. This is not all, there are some other big projects completed in Rust, for example, Piston, Zinc, and Maidsafe.

Learning Rust at this time and creating a mobile app will put you in the driving seat. Rust has the potential to take over C and C++ in near future.

Key features:

Not an easy language to learn.
Safer than most of the other languages.
It is fast.
It can be used to create a whole lot of applications in different fields.
Cargo, the build system, is very famous among developers.
Developers are in love with Rust.
Resources

Rust by example.

Introduction to Rust.

A 30-minute introduction to Rust.

SQL

Structured Query Language (SQL) is a programming language that is used for managing relational database management systems, database analytics, and for data processing.

SQL is not a language that is used for developing mobile apps but it supports applications.

Mobile apps where you have to access data from the server, SQL will be used. Essentially, it is the single language that will be integrated with most of the mobile apps. Learning SQL is, therefore, crucial.

ey features:

The best thing about SQL is that it doesn't require any coding.
It is portable and works on all devices.
One of the easiest languages to learn.

SQL standards make it even easier to understand and manage databases.

Works as a programming language and interactive language.

Both client and server side language.

Smoothly integrates with Java.

Resources

Free beginner course by SQL course.

Learn SQL free course by Code Academy.

SQL Zoo.

You've got to understand that most consumers begins their search experiences on on their mobile devices, and not on their computers. Therefore, you need to build mobile apps that caters to these consumers.

Create an amazing app icon too.

Then you've it. The thirteen programming languages for developing a mobile app, which one will you choose?

No idea…

Let me make it easier for you.

I'd recommend using (or learning) either Swift or BuildFire.js. Why?

These are the two programming languages that will redefine the future of programming – sooner or later.

If you choose to hire a professional mobile app developer, conduct a proper research, and hire someone who will understand your idea and goal, and design an app that communicates clearly with your target audience.

If You have a few moments, I would appreciate a review on Amazon, if You found your new book useful in any way.

Enjoy *!*

PS: sure the target is correct, take a look at my other published book, You should like it ->

LEARN PYTHON 3

" Practical course for beginners to programming in one week. A complete introduction guide to learn Python, step by step, with examples, tips & tricks and simple exercises, for everybody "

© Copyright 2019 by **WILLIAM GRAY**
All rights reserved

Printed in Great Britain
by Amazon